When I became ill with depression, Satan attacked our entire family. It took everything we had to fight this battle but We knew...

It's Too Soon To Give Up

By
Harry and Cheryl Salem II

Unless otherwise indicated, all Scripture quotations are taken from the *King James Version* of the Bible.

It's Too Soon To Give Up!
ISBN 1-890370-02-9
Copyright © 1998
Harry and Cheryl Salem
P.O. Box 701287
Tulsa, Oklahoma 74170

Acknowledgements

We want to especiallly thank Brenda Irvin who gave of her time for months to help us get our depression story on paper. May God multiply all your seeds sown into this ministry back to you one hundred fold. we love you.

Vicki Case, you have been a precious friend to us. We thank you and love you for your gift of writing and organizing the manuscript into the wonderful testimony it has turned out to be.

Contents

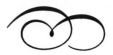

1

The Attack

"Whoever is in here is not me," I told Harry in a lifeless voice. "I have gone somewhere else and I don't even know who this person is inside me. This person is not me. I don't know how she got inside of me or where she came from."

I was the "choose to be happy" girl...the one who was full of energy. I was the "faith" girl. When I sank into depression that faithful, fun, energetic person left...she went somewhere else...and I became a different person.

I couldn't understand how this could happen to me. Before when Satan had put a mountain in front of me, God had removed it. I'd spent most of my life trying to help people believe God for miracles in their lives! Yet, here I was facing an immovable wall of depression and my miracle was no where to be found.

The first thing I noticed when I became ill was that I felt an unexplainable listlessness. I couldn't force myself to be energetic or excited about life. I didn't look forward to anything. This was not me. I had always been full of anticipation over each new ministry experience I had planned.

At first, no one noticed my condition. Harry was busy with his work and I was caring for the children. I knew I wasn't feeling like my old self but I attributed it to the stress I had been under. I was sure that I would get better.

I also hid a lot of these early feelings of depression from Harry and the children. For ten years, I was an abuse victim; I had learned well how to mask my true feelings. I allowed people to see only the positive side. I didn't want to worry anyone.

I was like many women; I had carved out a place for myself in our family that had everyone depending on me. I was the one my husband leaned on...the one who met the needs of my children. It was definitely not part of our family picture for me to be sick. I had trained everyone around me to depend on me...not the other way around.

My condition grew worse as the weeks passed. Harry began to notice my change of attitude. I could no longer hide my feelings from him. He would come home and say, "Honey, what's wrong?" I just couldn't describe how I felt. I would respond, "I don't know what's wrong. If I knew I would tell you." I wasn't trying to be disagreeable, I honestly didn't know what was wrong with me other than I felt so down.

There was such a heaviness...like a big weight on my body. I had to force myself to do my normal activities. I didn't want to do anything. I was the most exhausted person on earth. I had to force myself to do everything. It took all the emotional energy I had just to perform daily family functions and minister on the road.

Soon I began to have excruciating migraine headaches. The headaches were so severe that it felt as if my head was splitting wide open. I would find myself holding my head in my hands weeping uncontrollably... begging for someone to please help me. Much of the time, my head hurt so badly that I couldn't stand the light. When I came home from ministering I went into our bedroom and pulled the blinds. It was more comfortable for me to be in the dark.

I retreated from everyone the moment I got home...even though only hours before I had ministered under a rich anointing from God. I thought about how Elijah must have felt. Remember the story of the Juniper Tree? After one of his greatest campaigns where God had used Elijah to slaughter the prophets of Baal, he tells the Lord of his discouragement. In I Kings 19:4, Elijah sat down under a Juniper tree and told the Lord,

> *"I've had enough. Take away my life. I've got to die sometime, and it might as well be now."* Living Bible.

In one moment Elijah was greatly used of God...in the next he was at his lowest ebb. God loved Elijah, just as He loved me and He patiently held me in the palm of His hand and cared for me...and taught me new spiritual lessons.

Unexplainedly, the pounds began to fall off my body. When I looked into the mirror my eyes looked hauntingly empty. Harry became more and more alarmed as he watched my weight drop until I had lost twenty pounds. My eyes became so sunken; I could barely stand to look at my face in the mirror. I was eating but the pounds kept falling off. I looked as if I was anorexic...like walking death.

My body was so out of control that it couldn't seem to hold onto any weight. I could virtually feel my body losing weight. I hid the weight loss by wearing smaller clothes and turtleneck sweaters to hide my neck. I covered my gray colored skin with makeup. When I competed in the Miss America Pageant I learned many ways to hide the flaws in a person's appearance.

Each new day I made my positive confession of faith, "Father God, this is the day I will be well again. This is the day I will sing again." I became more and more aware of how serious my problem was each time I weighed myself.

Every morning, I said expectantly, "O.K., I ate a huge dinner last night, I know I've gained weight today." My spirits would plummet when the scales showed that I had not only not gained any weight...I had actually lost a half pound...or a pound! This was all in spite of the fact that Harry bought huge bags of groceries with high fat foods home to me. He brought the highest calorie take-out foods he could find. Still, we couldn't stop the weight loss. I knew then that this was definitely a spiritual problem because it just didn't make sense in the natural.

Inside my body, my blood was racing ninety miles an hour...as if I was running a race even when I was sitting still or trying to sleep. It was almost impossible to sleep at night because everything in me was racing. Every nerve in my body felt exposed. I was so exhausted that I couldn't rest.

Harry did everything he could to help me but he was becoming more and more perplexed and impatient by what he saw. It was hard for me to make him understand what I was experiencing...because I had never gone through anything like this and it wasn't something I could explain well.

I did such a good job hiding my condition that no one knew how depressed I was...except Harry. When I was ministering the anointing flowed, lifting and carrying me through the service but when I walked off stage I collapsed. I could minister but it was only an outward appearance... everything on the inside of me was dying.

Spiritually, I questioned God over and over. I had experienced so many healings in my life that were so much bigger than this. God had moved mountains in my life! *Where was God?*

I gave every ounce of energy I had to receiving my healing. I was exhausted from fighting one onslaught of attack after the other. I thought, "If I refuse to be moved by what I'm seeing in the natural Satan will be defeated and leave." But nothing seemed to work. In the natural, I could see no change in my condition. I wondered if there was something wrong with my faith.

I would ask Harry over and over again, *"Why can't I connect my faith? I know I am doing everything I know to do. I am praying, reading, confessing the Word, and believing, but this thing is not moving. What's wrong?"* I couldn't find an answer. I fell into self condemnation.

The days passed and turned into months and still I was no better. I was so despondent and worn out that I began to give up living on this earth. "Father God, I just don't want to stay here. I want to come and be with you. I'm so weary of fighting. Living each day is just too hard." In my mind the ultimate peace was in being with my Father God that I knew loved and cared for me so much.

Everything in me wanted to give up, although never before had I felt like quitting over anything. I felt like Elijah when he sat under the Juniper tree... discouraged and spent. I just wanted to go home to be with Jesus. I didn't feel suicidal. I just felt it would be much easier if I could go to my home in heaven. Thoughts of leaving began to fill my mind. If I could just slip down into the bathtub and ease away...or walk off the deep end of the pool and let the waters cover me up I would be at peace.

Then when I was at my lowest ebb...I lost my voice. As a singer this was one of the most unthinkable, devastating things that could have happened to me. It was almost the knockout blow! I couldn't even sing a lullaby to my precious baby girl...or sing the simplest songs that were no strain to my voice. My voice grew more raspy and hoarse sounding with each passing day. My vocal cords simply would not work. Nothing but raspy air came out when I tried to sing.

In faith, I forced myself to sing even though in the natural my voice sounded horrible. I would confess "Father, I am believing you for an anointing on my voice to minister to Your people. I believe with my faith that You have healed my voice." At first, when I began to sing my voice sounded weak and raspy, then after I sang the first few notes my normal voice would return...and for that service it would have a beautiful quality! I knew I had to take that step in faith even though in the natural there was no sign of healing anywhere.

I was so thankful to God for healing my voice but full of frustration because the healing didn't last. When I walked off the stage my sick voice would return and once again become raspy.

In desperation I cried out to God, *"What have I done wrong for this to come upon me? Have I not been out ministering enough? Have I done too much at home?"* My whole life I had reached out to God so he could tell me what I was doing wrong. This time I received no answers from Him in my mind...or my spirit.

I had gone to two doctors already who said I was depressed but Harry insisted that I go to see a spirit-filled doctor because he saw how physically drained I was; he knew I'd reached my lowest ebb. I can still remember sitting in the doctor's office, holding my head, crying because the pain was so intense.

The doctor reviewed my case...the weight loss, sleeplessness, voice loss and migraine headaches. He examined my throat and told me that my vocal cords had completely shut down...folded up.

"Cheryl, you have a chemical imbalance. You are depressed."

"You are wrong! That's just an excuse when you don't know what is wrong." I wasn't very nice to him but I was fighting for my life. I was full of anxiety.

He continued, "You are ill. Depression is the cause."

I countered, "No, it's not!"

He prescribed an antidepressant called Trazadone. This is a medication designed to treat the chemical imbalance that was causing the depression, voice loss, and headaches. (My final diagnosis was clinical depression, fibro mialga, chronic fatigue syndrome and connective tissue disease...one disease after another all within three months.) I saw several specialists before a diagnosis was made...but I fought them all. I absolutely refused to take the medicine.

I knew there was something drastically wrong with my body. I couldn't deny all the evidence. I had lost twenty pounds. I had lost my voice. I had severe migraine headaches. I had this awful heavy depression. I knew I needed to get well. I knew God wanted to heal me but I didn't think that He wanted to heal me through taking medicine. I wanted to have a physical problem. But not depression! I thought depression was like mental illness. I just couldn't make myself take the medicine. I felt confused by what was going on and I refused to let the doctor help me. I told everyone, "I'm not depressed! I'm happy; leave me alone." *I didn't understand that depression can be a medical problem, and that it can be physical.*

It tore at my heart that I was not able to care for our children the way I always had. I take a lot of pride in fulfilling my role as a mother. This is my special job and I feel an anointing to accomplish it. I desperately wanted to be my old self and care for my husband and family like I always had.

Every day I lost more of my joy...and I lost more of myself. My ministry was a constant reminder that my faith wasn't working. I had been happy all my life. I had never accepted moodiness, much less depression. I had always tried to cheer people up and taught "Choose to be happy." I wrote and sang songs about "Choose to be happy."

In the dark times, I challenged God, asking *"Is this ever going to get better?"* Every day I moved further down the road of despair...I was slipping away fast...going somewhere else. I felt as if I was six feet under water. I could see light, but I couldn't reach the surface to get a breath of air. I felt as if I was in a maze, and my spirit-man was up above it. My spirit-man could see the way out, but my natural-man was unable to get to the exit. Hard as I tried, I just could not find my way out! Depression was destroying me little by little. I had never felt the feelings of defeat in my whole life. Now, despair was pouring over me in torrents...covering me, drowning me.

I got to the point I felt so physically and emotionally depleted that at night I would beg God to take me home. I just didn't want to live any more.

In my mind, I knew that I had a beautiful, wonderful life. I had the greatest husband in the world and three wonderful children. I had everything I had ever dreamed of...and yet I longed to leave this earth.

The longer I struggled with depression the surer I was that it came from the very pit of hell. I know Satan's nature and this had his marks all over it. It is one of the strongest weapons he has at his disposal. The very nature of depression is like his nature. Depression is shame based and hidden from the view of most people. It is secret and almost covert...like Satan. Satan is always secretive in his attacks. It often takes us a long time to realize that he is behind the negative things we are experiencing.

I felt embarrassed that this was happening to me. Over the years I had fought and won many battles against Satan. I developed spiritual pride in my accomplishments. So besides the pain of my attack God began to teach me about spiritual pride. In Proverbs 16:18 it says, *"Pride goes before destruction and haughtiness before a fall." Amplified.* God always wants us to depend on and trust Him completely but sometimes our spiritual pride can block our connection to Him. Sometimes we ministers of the Gospel forget the things that we diligently teach to others.

When I was in the battle against Satan, it felt as if his arrows had invaded my entire body but James 4:7 says, *"Resist the devil and he will flee from you." Amplified.*

I couldn't rely on my emotions. I felt as if Satan was stalking me. I knew from experience that when I put my faith in God *I must believe more in what I couldn't see, than on what I could see and feel in the natural.* Although I didn't experience the answers to my prayers immediately, there was a tiny whisper in my spirit saying *"The answer is on the way."* I stand in faith...the devil does the fleeing!

In Daniel 10:11 an angel assured Daniel,

> *"O Daniel, greatly beloved of God," he said, "stand up and listen carefully to what I have to say to you, for God has sent me to you...Don't be frightened, Daniel, for your request has been heard in heaven and was answered the very first day you began to fast before the Lord and pray for understanding; that very day I was sent here to meet you. But for twenty-one days the mighty Evil spirit who overrules the kingdom of Persia blocked my way." Amplified.*

On the basis of the past encounters with Satan, I knew it was him I was fighting. I couldn't help thinking to myself "Satan must be real happy with himself." In my heart I vowed "Satan is not going to win this easily. This battle is not over until God and I win!"

In the end, God would use Harry, my husband, my partner, the man that I love deeply, to save my life. He would use his love, support, and dogged determination to work His miracle.

2

What God Joined Together...

Seeing Cheryl depressed was one of the hardest things I've ever experienced in my life! I couldn't believe she was the same person I knew and loved. The beautiful, happy woman I had met nine years ago had vanished. I didn't know where she went or how to get her back. I often remembered how happy she was the first time I saw her.

(I had no idea then that God would take our union and build a strong family ministry out of it.)

I met Cheryl for the first time when she ministered in one of our ORU Chapel services. She was a former Miss America and the ORU students really fell in love with her. As I watched and listened to her I saw her deep love and dedication to the Lord. Most importantly I saw the inner beauty He had given her.

When I walked back stage after the chapel service, there was quite a stir. The story of Cheryl's healing touched many of the students. Cheryl had been escorted to a waiting room in the back of the chapel to meet again with Richard and Lindsay Roberts. When she entered the room Richard took her by the arm and said a friend of his asked if he could meet her.

I introduced myself to her and explained in all the years I had been at ORU I'd never asked Richard for a favor. But that I had asked Richard if he could arrange a few minutes with her. I told her I was present at the chapel service and I knew everyone had enjoyed it. I told her I had felt she was a strong vessel of the Lord. But I also told her I saw something else: underneath that strong exterior there was a hurting, troubled person.

Cheryl couldn't believe my remark. I had no idea but at that time a stalker had been harassing her for weeks on end. Cheryl told me all her fears about being stalked, her security problems, and everything else. She asked if there was anything I could do and I said I had some friends that might be able to help her. I gave her my phone number and said to call me if she had any questions or needed anything.

Unfortunately, she lost my number! But I later learned my advice had been helpful. Eventually, the stalker stopped and her life began to get back to normal.

The next month, Cheryl was contacted by Richard and Lindsay Roberts to be on the show, and she flew to Tulsa. When she arrived the guest coordinator, who had been assigned to take care of her this trip, asked if Cheryl and her traveling companion would like to have lunch. When they went into the restaurant, I was there having lunch with some of the crew from the show. Cheryl asked me to join them.

I probably didn't act very interested in Cheryl but that was because I was seeing someone else. She told me later she didn't think too much about it. She had already decided she would probably be alone the rest of her life to fulfill the call of God on her life.

That night after the taping, Richard and Lindsay took her to dinner and asked if she would consider becoming a regular on the television program. They had a local pastor co-hosting with them and felt that a female singer would be a positive addition to the television family.

Their offer was very tempting to her, so they discussed her traveling schedule. They told her it didn't matter if she was gone some of the time, as long as she would be on the show when she was in town. She told them she would try it on a trial basis.

After moving into her apartment in Tulsa and getting comfortable, she started doing the show and began spending more and more time around the television staff. But we still hadn't had the opportunity to talk. Cheryl knew I was seeing someone but she thought that I might be interested in the outcome of the problem I had helped her with. Toward the end of the week I did call her. I was delighted to see her and we had a great talk.

In the course of the conversation, I told her how much I objected to women wearing lipstick, which came from boyhood memories of my Lebanese aunts. They would hug me, pinch my cheeks, and kiss me, leaving greasy, bright red lipstick all over my face. When Cheryl heard this she quietly got up and went into the kitchen, got a paper towel and wiped her lipstick off. She came back in the room and sat down on her end of the couch.

Nothing was said of this gesture, but I did not miss her intent. I told her later *that* was the moment I decided I was going to marry her. It wasn't that I was opposed to lipstick, but I was testing her to see how much of her comfort zone she was willing to give up to make me happy.

One year later, with a grin on my face, I handed her a tube of lipstick. "You have made your point," I smiled. The subject has never been mentioned again.

The realization that I wanted to marry Cheryl came as quite a shock to me, because I had decided that I would never find the right person. We talked for a little while longer, and nothing was ever said about our feelings for each other, but we both knew our lives were changing with every word we spoke.

I said I had to break off a relationship with someone else, and could not pursue our relationship until I did. I didn't touch her, hug her, or kiss her. I wanted to, but I wouldn't because of this other lady in my life. Cheryl said that was when she decided to marry me. She had never met anyone so loyal, and she needed that kind of loyalty in her life.

The next week Cheryl and I found ourselves traveling and working in the same city, so I met her at the airport to take her to dinner. A few miles down the road I pulled the car over and promptly told her that I wanted her to marry me. It was not in the form of a question, more of a statement. She said, "OK". I finally kissed her for the first time.

Cheryl went back on the road traveling and ministering, so we didn't see each other very much for the next few weeks. When she finally got back to Tulsa, my mother who was a widow and lived by herself, asked Cheryl if she would feel more comfortable living with her. Cheryl was thankful for the opportunity to get to know my mom. During that time, she fell in love with her. They developed a deep and lasting friendship over the next few weeks.

Cheryl and I were spending so little time together that we were beginning to wonder if we would ever see each other. I finally told her that if we didn't get our calenders together and come up with a date to get married, it might not ever happen! We decided on the only open weekend that both of us had for months. We ran off and got married. No one knew where we were or what we were up to and we didn't bother to tell them. I think we both needed to know that we had heard from God and that we were going to follow His direction.

Our schedules were so full that our honeymoon consisted of one wonderful night in Los Angeles. Full of excitement for our new lives together, we flew back to Tulsa and then Cheryl left for a ministry date.

3

A History of Miracles

Before I met and married Harry, God had performed many healing miracles for me. I learned early in my life that God would never fail me in the difficult moments of my life. I grew to have a strong, *stubborn* faith that God would take care of me in every way. When Satan attacked my life with depression, I couldn't understand why God didn't heal me the way He always had.

Even as a child, I spent hours searching my Bible to learn God's way of healing. I discovered that there are steps of faith to take in order to receive from God. Every time I took these steps God met my needs in a miraculous way.

When I began my journey with God all I knew was that He was a good God. I didn't really know if it was God's will to heal me but I was hungry to learn everything I could. This is how God taught me to receive from Him.

I grew up in rural Mississippi...in Choctaw County to be specific. We were dirt poor financially but very rich spiritually.

We were so poor that I can still remember pulling a Barbie doll out of the trash that had its arm chewed off. In my eyes, it was the most beautiful doll in the world. I didn't care if it was somebody else's "throw-away." No one knew what a thrill it was to have my very own doll. (Today Harry gives me a brand new Barbie doll every Christmas as a reminder of his love and also as a reminder of the miraculous things God has done in my life.)

Our family was in church every Sunday. In fact, we were there every Sunday morning, every Sunday night, and every Wednesday night. It didn't matter what you did the rest of the week; you had better be in church on Sunday. Our family was very musical and I sang with my sister and brothers as a family in our church. My church was a good church but it didn't teach physical healing.

I was healthy and happy until that terrible day when my life would abruptly change forever. My sister, my two brothers, and I were on our way to town to get tomato plants. It was garden planting time! We were all pretty excited to be going for an outing. We had gone about a mile when we spotted a parked car in front of a friend's house. We were traveling on such a narrow gravel road that we had to swerve to miss the parked car...there wasn't room to go anywhere else. We had just passed the car in our path when in a sickening moment we spotted an oncoming car. The car belonged to our next-door neighbors who had been out buying groceries. When the cars got to the top of a rise in the road, we hit head-on!

There was a terrible crashing sound of metal hitting metal and of smashed broken glass everywhere...the smell of oil and fuel. There was blood spattered on every side. When the sounds stopped there was the sound of quiet weeping and disbelief that spread over us like a blanket. The mother of our next-door neighbor's family was dead still sitting in the front seat. The impact of hitting another car head-on not only caused my face to hit the windshield, it drove the engine of our car through the dashboard where it landed right in my lap. I'll never forget how frightened and sick I felt when I regained consciousness and saw my left leg. My leg was crushed so badly above the knee, that the skin in the top and bottom touched as though someone had taken the bone out; there was no evidence of any bone above the knee!

When we finally arrived at the hospital, the doctors put over 100 stitches in my face and then just stopped counting. There were so many cuts they couldn't possibly count all the stitches! After they finished in the emergency room, a nurse gave me a mirror. When I looked in it my spirits sank; my face looked grotesque like something out of a horror movie.

The little girl that looked back at me in the mirror was ugly and defeated. In my pain, I desperately reached for God and He began to show me what real beauty was. He showed me that outward physical appearance does not mean as much to Him—or anyone else—as inner beauty. He told me, *"If you'll focus on the inside...I'll take care of the outside."*

I was only eleven years old but somehow God drew me to Himself. I began to spend hours with Him, letting Him feed me spiritually. Even at a young age I found my spirit grow strong in His presence. As I talked to Him with my child-like faith I began to change on the inside. In my mind and heart I began to see that God had the power and the desire to heal me.

Although I was attending our little country church, no one ever talked about healing. I asked my mama and daddy about it and they didn't know anything. As time passed, I sensed that if I was ever going to walk again only God could heal me. Somehow I *knew* He was the answer for me to be whole again. I developed a hunger to learn everything I could about healing from the Bible.

With my little heart full of faith, I went to the Lord with all the boldness I could muster and said, "God, I don't know how You do this kind of thing, but I want You to heal me." From the moment I asked Him to heal me, I believed He would.

I had child-like faith and I understood the principles involved. I understood that God is all-powerful and that He is like a father. I knew that Luke 11:13 says that if our fathers here on earth want to give us good things, then we should understand that our Heavenly Father wants to give us so much more! As I watched my earthly father and mother cry and weep as all four of their children lay hurting in that hospital after the accident, wanting us all well, I knew that God, my heavenly Father, wanted me well too.

That's the way I received my healing. Even though I was a child, my faith was strong enough to believe my heavenly Father for my healing. A cocoon of bone began to manifest itself, just wrapping up and down inside my left leg. At the end of three months, when they cut the body cast off and stood me up to examine my left leg, the doctors declared my recovery a miracle. They said the bone in my left leg was the strongest one in my entire body.

Because I was eleven years old and still growing, my right leg had grown almost two inches longer than my left one. I didn't mind...I was just happy to have two legs that would work. I didn't care if one was a little different from the other. I was thrilled to be able to walk.

School was starting soon, so Mama set about hemming the left leg of all my pants approximately two inches shorter than the right leg. And off to school I went. My friends said I was a cripple but I said I was a miracle. That's what made the difference—the way I saw myself and believed in myself, not the way they saw me.

At fourteen years of age, I asked Jesus into my heart as my Lord and my Savior. I had not fully accepted Jesus Christ as my Savior at the time of my healing. You see, at the time I grew up in the South; everybody went to church. I was in church at least three times every week so I knew a lot *about* God. I knew everything the Father had done for me by sending His only Son to die for me. I knew everything Jesus had done for me by dying on the cross for my sins. I didn't *know* the Father, and I didn't *know* Jesus.

It was then that God the Father began to speak in my heart and let me know, "You know all about Me, but you don't know Me. You know all about my son Jesus, but you don't know My Son Jesus."

Right then I had a personal encounter with the Father and I asked Him to be my Lord and my Savior. It was then that He began to work in my heart and to move inside me. I would need His strength in the future because that was not the end of my problems.

Three years later, when I was seventeen years old; a doctor told me that I would have problems later on in life. He was talking about how damaged the inside of my body was, along with my hips, as a result of the accident. Because of that damage, he feared that I would not be able to have any children.

Well, I had learned in the six years since my accident never to panic, just to go to God's Word and find what He has to say about the situation. So I searched through the books of Matthew, Mark, Luke, and John and found that one of the greatest works Jesus did was healing lame legs. When I saw that, I thought, "If Jesus will heal that man with a lame leg, He will heal me, too!"

As I began to see these principles of faith and grasp hold of them, I became more and more hungry to learn. Many times, I would just open the Bible at any point and start reading the

Word to myself. Then I decided to read it out loud because if I read it aloud I would hear it, and if I heard it, it would get down into my heart. Matthew 12:34 says, *"...out of the abundance of the heart the mouth speaks." King James.*

As I did this, I discovered that this is the way it goes: You get the Word of God down in your heart, and then it comes out of your mouth, and when it comes out of your mouth, it gets in your ears. You can get a good cycle of faith going in your life just by letting your ears hear the Word and your mouth saying it. I knew that if I wanted my body healed; I had to have faith. Romans 10:17 says that *"...faith cometh by hearing and hearing by the word of God." King James.* So I read the Bible out loud so that I could hear the word and get my faith to come to me!!

I especially liked to read the Bible on the days when the devil was hanging around and would not leave me alone. I had to show him who was boss; so on those days I would say, "Devil, just pull up a chair. I believe I will read to you today." I would open the Bible and I'd start reading to him. He didn't like that very much, so I'd read some more. Then I would read louder and louder and louder and it wouldn't be very long before he left. The devil didn't like the Word of God then, and he still doesn't like it!

My faith grew stronger and stronger because I was reading the Word and hearing the Word. About six weeks passed with my doing this. Then the fateful day came.

I had been teaching piano lessons for a while when the mother of one of my students asked if I wanted to attend a meeting in which an evangelist named Kenneth Hagin was going to be speaking on faith. I had never heard of him (no one in my little church knew him) but when he came to town, I went to hear him. I had never been to a service like that one. It seemed as though everyone was full of faith and hungry and ready for God to move in their lives. I believe God's anointing was already on the place before we ever even did anything.

At the end of the service, Brother Hagin asked if anybody in the audience wanted to receive their healing. Well, I was ready! I went right down to the front of the auditorium where many of the people were standing in line waiting for Brother Hagin to lay his hands on them and pray for them.

As I stood there, I heard Brother Hagin say, "Just get your mind and your eyes and ears off of everybody, including yourself. Just close your eyes and center on the Father." As I did what Brother Hagin suggested, I saw the Father sitting on the throne with His son Jesus beside Him. As I saw them in my spirit, I said, "Lord, I just want You to give me anything and everything You want me to have." As soon as I said that, I began to feel the arms of God the Father and Jesus the Son as they reached out to me. They were different arms, but the same person—it was as if they were one. They reached out, brought me up into their arms and just whispered into my ear. "Child, We've been waiting for you." When the Lord spoke those words to me, just like that, my left leg grew out to the same length as my right leg!

For years my mama hemmed one pant leg shorter than the other so my limping wouldn't be as noticeable. Mama didn't want people to criticize me and treat me harshly. My faith leaped as I looked down at my pant leg. I was standing there in that meeting with my navy pants on...there was one pant leg shorter than the other. God revealed my healing to everyone. I no longer had one leg shorter than another...I had one pant leg shorter than another! I was able to see my miracle before my eyes as I looked down at my mother's hemmed up pant leg.

That was when it all started happening for me. Although I

had never lifted my hands in a service, I lifted them then because it just felt like the thing to do. Suddenly I began to speak in another language. I thought, "Father, You've given just me a whole precious gift." I thought I was the only one who had this gift. I didn't know that many thousands of others had it too! Later I found out that I had received an infilling of the Holy Ghost, one of the Holy Trinity, and that He was just for me, as He is just for you and each of God's children.

God has always been there for me in the healing moments of my life but when Satan attacked me with depression, I couldn't seem to find Him. I was ill but all anyone could see were the outward signs of the weight loss...the migraine headaches...the voice loss. I didn't have one leg shorter than the other. This was new ground for me. I used my faith...I believed God but I found out that there is a difference in this kind of illness. Before when I believed God...even as a child...my mind was functioning in a healthy way. Now Satan had attacked my mind by making it physically imbalanced...he hit me in an area where it was harder to fight back. The mind connects our faith and all of our actions...when it isn't physically functioning properly our faith can become disconnected. This is why we need to have faith people in our lives. There may be a time when we need their faith to help us receive our healing. It's not that my faith wasn't there—not at all! It was just disconnected for a time. This is where someone else can come in with intercession and "stand in the gap" and be the "re-connector" for our faith until we receive our miracle.

One thing I have learned in my journey of healings is that God does not cause illness but *He will use it for good.* What the devil means for bad, God will use for good. In my case, He used the situation to pull our family closer together than we had ever been before. He will take any curse Satan throws at us and turn it into a blessing if we will only trust Him. Deuteronomy 23:5 says, *"...but the Lord your God turned the curse into a blessing to you, because the Lord your God loves you."* *Amplified.*

My husband Harry saved my life. God allowed me to see how tough my husband was...how tenacious he was...how I was one of his main priorities...how dedicated he was...how protective he was of the children and of me. God also used this time to work a miracle in Harry's life. Where before he had known God but didn't really *know* him, his faith grew by leaps and bounds and he not only became a powerful spiritual leader of our family but an anointed minister.

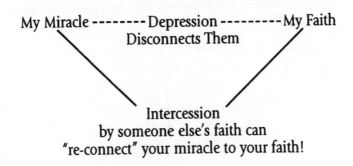

My Miracle - - - - - - - - Depression - - - - - - - - - My Faith
Disconnects Them

Intercession
by someone else's faith can
"re-connect" your miracle to your faith!

4

A Birthright of "Being Tough"

"Don't be a sucker for anybody." Those were the last words my dad ever spoke to me. In my mind, if I fell short of his direction, I was a failure. Even as a young boy, I felt tremendous pressure on me to be successful and tough. I had to be a man, no matter what. My father told me not to show my feelings. He told me I should never talk about my feelings. He said that if I let anybody know how I felt it was a sign of weakness. I shouldn't let anyone get close to me. As a child, he had a profound influence on me. He was my whole world.

Then at the age of nine years old my entire life changed. Without warning, my father was stricken with leukemia and taken to the hospital. My family turned to God in our pain and devastation...searching for answers.

My family watched Oral Roberts on television at the hospital. One day while we were watching his program, he said, "Place your hand on the television set as a point of contact for your faith" and so we all joined hands and believed God for my father's healing. It gave us a great deal of comfort to know that Oral was there for us. We began to send our prayer requests to him believing that God would give us a miracle.

One day late in October of 1968 my father received an unexpected telephone call from Oral Roberts. They talked for a few moments and then Oral prayed for my father's healing. Then Oral asked my father if he would like to rededicate his life to the Lord. He said, "Yes, I would like that very much." Ten days later my father died.

Our whole family was shattered by our loss. My father was a powerful man and when he died he left a big hole in all our lives. Even in our pain we felt the comfort of God's love for us, just knowing my father was in heaven.

Even though I was just a child when my father died, he meant the world to me. My father was such an important part of my life that when he died I felt as if a part of me died too. I felt tremendous pain and emptiness when I lost my father. My mind was tormented by thoughts and feelings that history would repeat itself.

While growing up, my father was a great father to me. I knew he loved me and was proud that I was his son. I just wish I had had the time to get to know my father better. Most of my life my father worked long hard hours. He was an excellent provider. He worked six days a week. Many days he worked from 8:00 a.m. to 9:30 p.m. The only time I saw him was if my mom would take me to visit him at work. He worked through lunches, dinners, holidays, and anniversaries. He didn't think anything about it. That was his nature.

My dad came from a long line of hard workers. For generations, the men in our family have had a strong work ethic. Even when he was a little boy his father made him work in the family grocery store instead of playing baseball in the sandlot.

While we were in church on Sunday my father was outside mowing the church lawn. That was his way of doing something good for the church. It was his way of participating...and having a relationship with God.

The son of a Lebanese immigrant, my father learned to provide for his family above all else. If he provided for his family he was a good father. His parents told him that if he wasn't financially successful he wasn't much of a man.

Dad joined the Marines when the war came. He was barely 17 years old but he took pride in his self discipline and strong work ethic. Thank God for men who served in the armed forces. It shows what a strong person he was.

My father was a depression child. Work was difficult to get. People were starving in the streets. You worked whenever you could and wherever you could and as long as they would let you.

My mom was very understanding. They both did what they thought was right and necessary for the family. He didn't work hard because he wanted to hurt his children. He definitely didn't work hard because he didn't care. He did it to provide for his family.

He was so busy working hard that he didn't hear that still small voice that wanted to guide his life...that voice that wanted to tell him how to function according to God's way...not his.

You might be thinking "What is so bad about a man who wants to provide the best for his family"? Nothing. But that's not enough. You see I wish my father could have understood this one thing. I needed him to have an intimate relationship with me more than to give me toys. I would have much rather had him be home with me playing catch with an old baseball glove.

Even at this young age my father groomed me to be successful in business. When I was at the car dealership, he told me to watch and listen to what was going on around me. One time he told me to sit by the back door and watch what was going out the door. He let me help him around the dealership whenever he could.

My father was a workaholic. A workaholic is the same as an alcoholic...they both have an addictive spirit. That spirit is a deception of Satan. He tells us that the way to happiness is through things.

I want you to know I had the utmost respect for my father and loved him immensely...but his workaholism impacted my life for years to come.

I followed in his footsteps when I grew up. At 26 years old I was the Vice-President of the Oral Roberts Evangelistic Association, Vice-President of buildings and grounds and head of Oral Roberts television. I was responsible for a large number of employees. I became so stressed that I developed heart problems. I didn't realize it but I was walking in my father's footsteps.

Even though I was working hard, God was preparing me to work in the ministry.

During all the years I was with the Oral Roberts Evangelistic Association, I listened to countless anointed messages both from Oral and Richard Roberts as well as many great guest ministers. Although I worshipped God at a distance then...I know now He was filling my mind and spirit with His Word.

While I was growing up, I felt determined to be strong like my dad. Because of what he told me before he died it was difficult for me to trust anyone. I was always questioning people's motives. Did they want to hurt me?

I stressed myself out a lot and often used food that was not good for me to numb my feelings. I lived to eat pizza and foods that were high in fat. When I did that it added to the stress my body was already experiencing. My cholesterol was over 500. My toughness was definitely damaging my health.

I didn't smile. I can still remember my wife, Cheryl, asking me if I would please smile in our family pictures. I said, "I *am* smiling." In my mind I was smiling! Then I remembered my dad telling me, "Don't you smile in any pictures." I didn't know what he meant. I now know that he was saying, "Don't smile and show your teeth that are missing." I was eight years old with no front teeth but I misunderstood what he said to me as a little boy and made it a way of life!

My mother raised me by herself and did the best she could to instill openness and sensitivity in me. It was difficult for me as a man to incorporate her teaching because the shadow of my powerful father fell over my life! It raised a lot of conflict in me. I received her teaching regarding good manners and other things. I questioned being open. It was contrary to what my father told me to do or so I thought.

A son looks up to his father...even if he is giving him information that is in err and can cause him pain. It takes a lot of years to break down those walls. It is only through the life-changing love of Jesus Christ that the pain from the past is healed.

I thought I had to be the toughest man alive. I could never let my emotions get the best of me. I could never let my guard down. Above all I should never let anyone know I hurt or that I was in trouble. I had to keep my problems to myself. My identity as a man was at stake. My heritage as a strong middle eastern man was at stake. I was the son of a man who told me never to be weak or in his words *"a sucker."* My heritage was to be tough.

I transferred my feelings of distrust to my relationship with God. I could not trust anyone, so I did not have a relationship of trust with Him. I felt suspicious, untrusting, and unwilling to come too close to God for fear of being hurt. He might ask me to do something that I didn't want to do. I didn't confess my sins because I didn't want God to know too much about me. He might use it against me. Does this sound a little like Jonah? The belly of my whale was waiting for me!

My *"tough"* code of behavior was not just for people...it was for God, too! Deep down I knew that God knew everything I felt, did, or was going through but I still resisted Him. God was up in heaven and I consented to let Him take care of me from a distance. I thought it would be a personal imposition to call on Him for a personal need of mine. I was a strong man...I could handle the situation no matter what. Besides, in my mind, God had so many other needy people to help...starving children, and people with terminal illnesses, people that couldn't help themselves!!

It wasn't until I experienced a series of crisis in my life that I began to discover my true identity and heritage. Don't get me wrong. Jesus was my Savior but He wasn't the Lord of my life. I hadn't let Him be the Lord of my life because I would not let down the protective walls or guard I had built around myself. These walls prevented me from letting Him come into my heart in a personal way. I didn't want to give up *control*! Control is a big issue with a so-called strong man!

I had let just enough of Him in to call Him my Savior...but not enough to let Him be my leader. I hadn't let him be my best friend or Father, a motivating force in my life. I discovered that I had received my *true heritage* when my Savior died for me two thousand years ago...not when I was a little boy. My inheritance is the Kingdom of Heaven not a car dealership in Michigan. My true identity is that of husband, daddy, and servant...not some false person with walls higher than the Empire State Building. I am a man with feelings and I can share them with others and not be less of a man.

God prepared Moses for an important mission that lay ahead by having him raised in the palace at the feet of military strategists. God sowed life lessons of strength and determination of character in me and then added years of sitting under some of the greatest teachers in the ministry so that I would be prepared to accomplish His work. Moses knew little of the God of his heritage until he spoke to the God of the burning bush. I too, resisted knowing God personally...until He got my attention and moved in a mighty way in my life...just as He did with Moses.

For so long I wanted God to send me a burning bush just as He did for Moses. I felt that I deserved it! I deserved *a great big sign* just like Moses. One day while I was talking and sharing with God how I felt He should "send me a burning bush" He revealed to me that He sent me something so much greater than a burning bush! He sent me His Son, Jesus, to die on the cross *just for me!*

5

And They Became One Flesh

Cheryl and I came from completely different backgrounds. It is truly one of God's greatest miracles when he joins a man and a woman together and they become one. God didn't cause Cheryl's depression but He certainly used it to do a great work in our lives. There is a saying that "When the going gets tough...the tough get going." That was certainly true in our battle against depression. First, God had to draw us closer together to fight this battle and to start a ministry.

"Therefore a man shall leave his father and his mother and shall become united and cleave to his wife, and they shall become one flesh." Genesis 2:24

For several weeks, we didn't tell anyone but family that we were married. God had moved quickly in our lives to bring us together and I wasn't sure how people would respond to our marriage.

My father had always told me to keep my personal business private. "Harry, don't be a sucker for anyone in life. You are the head of the household. You're the man," he warned me just before he died. I was 10 years old and I felt this enormous burden placed on my shoulders. My father didn't mean to say anything to me that would be harmful but those words changed the way I lived my life for years. It was very difficult for me to trust people after that.

Now the words of my father echoed in my head, "Don't let anybody know anything. Don't trust anybody because people will hurt you." So even though Jesus lived in my heart and I had just experienced a miracle, I kept my affairs very private. I didn't want anyone to hurt us.

My father was a good man. I had a tremendous admiration for him. He was a successful businessman...he became President of the Automobile Association of Michigan at a young age. He worked 14 hours a day, six days a week! He often worked on Sundays, too. He provided well for his family but he never had time to spend with us. I felt abandoned when he died.

From the time we arrived home from our brief honeymoon our lives were a whirlwind of activity. Cheryl was a former Miss America and was traveling a lot. I was working for the Oral Roberts Ministry and traveling a lot. She was in the North. I was in the South. I was in the East. She was in the West. We were spending our time in the ministry...giving and giving and giving.

My responsibilities with the ministry were growing. I was responsible for a large budget. I was responsible for television and a lot of what the ministry was doing. We had just gotten married but we saw very little of each other. We took off in separate directions.

In July we were finally able to schedule a three day vacation. We had an amazing time. It was great to relax together. We spent time talking and laughing and just enjoying each other. As a result of our time together we conceived a baby. It happened sooner than we expected but we were both tremendously excited! Having a family was a high priority in both of our lives. We only had one problem. Very few people knew we had gotten married. I told Cheryl, "We better tell everybody...soon!"

We had to live our secrecy down. I spent a lot of time holding our marriage certificate up with the May 10 date on it assuring people of our wedding date. Soon the excitement died down and we looked with anticipation at the approaching birth of our baby. Cheryl felt good all during her pregnancy and was able to continue to travel. We were sure all was well.

True to what my father had taught me, I became Cheryl's protector. In Tulsa, while she was pregnant, I would walk in front of her in shopping malls. If someone bumped her I would jump to her defense. I thought that it was my responsibility to protect her.

Cheryl's background was completely different from mine. She was trusting and free-spirited. It was difficult to protect her. I wasn't sure how to handle our differences. Usually, I handled them with anger.

The months passed and our excitement grew over the prospect of having a new baby. Before we knew it, it was time to go to the hospital. Cheryl's pregnancy had been perfectly normal. There was no sign of anything wrong until she went into labor. When Little Harry was born we discovered all had not been well. Two weeks earlier Harry had a bowel movement in the womb. It caused toxin in the water and he drank poisonous water for two weeks. When he was born he was green from all the infection that was in the water. The doctors told us that he shouldn't have survived the toxicity. We thanked God that he had protected and delivered our precious baby out of the hands of the enemy! (Green but alive!)

Cheryl enjoyed staying home and playing with the baby for

a couple of months, but then she felt God calling her to minister. When she went back on the road I became more and more firm in my efforts to protect her. I made her promise, "When you get off the plane I want you to call me." I just wanted to know that she was OK. I worried when she was away from me and I wanted to take care of her. Cheryl had come from a family that had not functioned that way. She had always been free to drive across the country by herself. They never asked her to call when she got there. They had always said, "We'll see you when you get back." They completely trusted Cheryl (and the Lord) to take care of herself.

As much as Cheryl loved me, she felt controlled by my protectiveness and dreaded making those calls. During those trips, she didn't like talking to me because I acted so concerned, which to her seemed like disapproval and anger most of the time. She would pray, "Oh, God, do I have to call him? He makes me feels so bad when I'm not there."

Finally, Cheryl prayed the prayer of relinquishment and put her faith into action. She prayed, "Lord, you gave me this man and if he cannot stand my traveling and you have called me to do this, then you have to deal with him and change his heart. If this doesn't happen I'm going to have to give up my calling. I put it in Your Hands." She agreed with the lady she traveled with saying, "Lord, speak to him or speak to me...so we can both be happy and not have this stressful thing between us."

Meanwhile, I felt my heart harden on the subject. It was difficult for me to think about her being gone.

What I didn't know was that Cheryl had talked to God about our problem. Later that year the Lord spoke to me in a Norvel Hayes meeting in California while Cheryl was in the East ministering, "If Cheryl is called to a ministry and you don't let her do her ministry, you'll be standing before Me."

The Lord had never spoken so clearly to me. That night I called her and said, "OK. Go." It was the hardest thing I ever did. But God has blessed our lives through the ministry. I didn't realize it then but He was preparing the way for our ministry together by helping us work together as a team and see that He had His hand on our lives.

This was a perfect example of being obedient but not willing. I obeyed God but I still wasn't nice about it. I didn't make it easy on her in any way. I still made her pay for every trip emotionally!

I had to learn to be *willing* and *obedient* to God. As the years progressed I became *willing* and *obedient;* I finally let God soften my heart. I stopped punishing Cheryl emotionally and let her enjoy the call of God on her life but not without her coming off the road alone and us joining together as a family.

We've learned it's not the problems that confront you in your life...everyone has problems...it is what you do with them. We are two very strong people and that is the way God made us. When we used Christian principles to solve our problems it drew us close and we became "One Flesh."

It was the strength of our union that helped us fight off the attack of Satan on our family. And it was the strength of our union that made both of us trust God enough to stop doing what we were doing separately and start doing what God called us to do *together*!

6

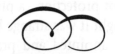

Our Children...Blessings From the Lord

When I had my first accident the doctor told me that I might never have any children. This was a false accusation from Satan. Today, Harry and I have three beautiful children. It wasn't without a struggle though because Satan attacked each one of our children just as he attacked me with depression. Just because Satan attacks you it does not mean he is victorious. Here's how God blessed us with children in spite of Satan's attacks.

I loved being a mother to Lil' Harry. My life was full with the ministry and a young child. It was a challenge for me to become a good parent but Lil' Harry was a real joy to us. When he was three years old he began talking about wanting a brother. Of course he didn't know we had been thinking the same thing. Our old excitement over thinking about a new baby returned and we began to make plans. I scheduled my pregnancy when the speaking engagements weren't as full.

I became pregnant on schedule...and there were no physical problems. I was totally unaware that our family was about to experience an attack from Satan on our lives. Several weeks before Roman was born the Lord woke me up and said, "Go anoint all of your doors and all of your windows. Put a hedge of protection...a prayer cover over all of your family." I thought it was strange because I always kept the house and cars anointed and prayed over but I had learned through the years to be obedient to God's voice. I anointed them all again.

Three weeks later I gave birth to our second child. Roman was born healthy except for having sucked some amniotic fluid in his lungs. He would have to stay in the hospital two extra days. I was still high from all the excitement when Harry received a telephone call from the police. Roman was one day old. The police wanted Harry to come to the station.

"Do any of these women look familiar?" Astonished, Harry said, "Yes, they all look like my wife. They are all brunettes. They're all about 35 years old. They're all about 5'7". *And that happens to be my wife and that is our office address.*" The sergeant, seeing the shocked look on Harry's face, explained. "We have arrested a stalker who abducted two women with the intent of raping one and then killing them both. They both got away and came to us. Your wife would have been next on his list!"

Harry was shocked that his wife and family had been in such danger. He was thankful that God had protected us but it gave him a new awareness of the potential dangers his family might be subject to.

Even though the stalker went to prison Harry's male instincts said to cover me up...bring me closer. He didn't tell me about the incident at the time because he didn't want me walking around looking over my shoulder. What he didn't know was that I had long ago made a decision not to operate in fear. At that time Harry's way of handling things was much different from mine. I am a free spirit, like a butterfly and he smothered my wings and wouldn't let me fly because he was protecting me!

Harry and I considered our children a blessing from the Lord. We enjoyed our children so much that when Roman was 2 1/2 years old we decided to complete our family by having another child.

I became pregnant but ten weeks into the pregnancy I lost our little baby through a miscarriage. It was a heartbreaking, terrible thing to experience. I was full of pain over our loss but I knew that our child was in heaven with our Heavenly Father.

Both Harry and I felt that it was an attack on our entire family. Once again Satan attacked one of our children. He always attacks what he thinks will hurt us both. We both came to see that the attacks were going to be great on our lives and the lives of our family!

Later Harry told me how full of grief he was...but how he tried to stay strong for me. He told me, "I didn't allow myself to grieve. I didn't know how. I didn't think that it was the manly thing to do."

When we got home from the hospital Harry told Lil' Harry about our baby. "Son, I need to tell you that Mommy's baby is no longer in her tummy." He had braced himself, thinking that tears would follow. Instead, Lil' Harry asked in a matter of fact way, "What's the baby's name?" It was a powerful question that took Harry completely by surprise. Harry told him that we hadn't named it. Lil' Harry remembered what we had told him about heaven and he reasoned, "If we are going to see the baby in heaven, aren't we supposed to know the baby's name?"

Lil' Harry's faith touched a chord deep inside Harry. He choked up. The tears ran down his face. Harry told me that it was the faith of his little boy that pulled him through. All of a sudden Harry *understood* that it was OK to have feelings...to grieve. Our family named the baby Malachi Charlie because Malachi means God's messenger and Charlie was Harry's grandfather's name. We didn't know if it was a boy or a girl so we thought "Mali" would work for either!

When Harry allowed himself to feel the pain of our loss, God began leading Harry to help other men who have experienced the same thing. Most men have no idea that it's OK to grieve much less HOW to grieve. Men will come up to Harry who have lost babies and say, "Well, my wife's doing real good." Harry tries to help them focus on themselves. He asks them,

"But how are YOU doing?" From his experience he knows men hurt too.

"Well, we're all right." He doesn't accept their attempt to glaze over the surface.

"No, it was your baby, too. Maybe it was your little boy. You need to let your feelings come to the surface. Don't let them cause a wound on your heart!"

"Well, you know I just haven't had anybody to talk to about it."

Men have to grieve too. I'm not talking about the spirit of grief that leads you down a destructive path but Godly grief that lets God *heal* the hurt instead.

Remember in I Peter 2:9 God brings all things out of darkness (out of secrets, out of hiding, out of the closet) into His Heavenly healing light. God doesn't want you to cover up and hide. He wants you to run to Him as your Father, jump up in His lap, and let Him heal your wounds!

7

This Baby Will Live and Not Die and Declare the Works of the Lord!

Cheryl and I really wanted a third child so shortly after her miscarriage we conceived another child. When Cheryl was ten weeks into the pregnancy, I was in California and Cheryl was on the East Coast at a church in Virginia Beach. We decided to join together at Melodyland in Anaheim, California and fly back home together. Two days later, Cheryl left for Seattle by way of Dallas. (We have decided when the "rapture" comes we will probably have to go through Dallas on the way up!) I was still in Tulsa when I received an emergency phone call. They patched in the police radio from the ambulance. It was the ambulance attendant.

"Are you Mr. Salem?"

"Yes."

"Is Cheryl Salem your wife?"

"Yes."

"Well, we have her in our ambulance. She is hemorrhaging and we don't know why. You need to get to Northridge

Hospital right away."

Then he hung up. No details at all. Nothing. (Cheryl would say, "Just like a man, no details, just the 'headlines!') I didn't even have time to tell them that my wife was pregnant. They had taken her right off the airplane and put her in the ambulance.

My world started coming to an end. My immediate thought was that I was going to lose her. I thought, "She's been abused, she's been divorced, she's had two babies. Lately, I had been under so much stress at work I had put her through hell on earth on a daily basis." I had felt the weight of the ministry on my shoulders...that if the ministry failed it would be my fault. Sometimes my stress came out on her, most of the time really....

Childhood memories of my mother rearing me as a single parent surfaced. I feared "I'm going to have to raise two boys by myself. Just like my mother raised me. Here we go, the whole cycle again. Satan began to whisper lies to me "you're going to lose the baby. You're going to lose your wife. Your boys are going to lose their mother. You're going to lose your family."

For a moment, Satan had me on the run. Years of listening to strong teaching and being in and around the ministry came to my mind. "No." I reasoned. "That's my natural man speaking to me. I know my wife. I know she's down there believing. I'm going to agree with her right now." In that moment the strength of our relationship came through. Through our years together, we learned how each other would react in crisis. First the natural...what's happening? Then the supernatural...we can stop it with our faith!

At that moment Cheryl was on her way to the hospital. Cheryl remembers it this way. "I didn't start to bleed like a normal miscarriage. I began hemorrhaging horribly. I was covered with blood from my waist to my feet! It was puddling up on the floor. I passed a clot bigger than a coffee cup which I wouldn't give up to the ambulance driver. (This clot was actually bigger than the fetus from my previous miscarriage.) Within five minutes the paramedics were there and I was in the ambulance. My natural man said, 'This is much worse than the miscarriage I just experienced.' But my spirit just would not let go. I refused to be deceived that quickly and that easily. My spirit man rose up on the inside and refused to let go. When we arrived at the hospital I was still bleeding and the nurses were changing bed pads quickly as each was soaked in a matter of minutes.

"An hour later I was still bleeding profusely. The doctor performed a pelvic examination. 'You've lost the baby and you're torn inside.' He said matter of factly. 'And you have a number of tumors on your ovaries. But you have definitely lost the baby.' Then he left. But in spite of all the negative evidence I just *knew that I knew* that God was going to save our baby.

"I refused to hear this negative report. I was still dealing with his words when a nurse, who was trying to comfort me, struck a nerve. She tried to console me by saying, 'This is the body's natural way to cleanse itself. It's not a baby anyway.' Well, that's all it took for my faith to kick into gear and for words of faith to pour out of my mouth! Up until that time I had been quiet. But when I heard the nurse saying such preposterous things, that were just not scripturally true, I couldn't let her continue with this misinformation. I sat straight up on the table and began to preach!

"Wait a minute. God knew this baby before it was ever in my body. He knew this baby the instant the sperm and the egg came together to form a human being. This baby has a spirit from the Father God. This baby has a job to do and a plan laid out for its

life. It has a will. And it has a way. God's way is living not dying. God's way is to overcome."

As well meaning as the nurse was, nobody was going to come and tell Cheryl that this wasn't God's baby. The nurse's face turned white. She backed up and said she was sorry. She would never tell another mother that!

When I arrived at the hospital and walked down the hall to Cheryl's room I heard my wife preaching to this nurse. She was sitting on the edge of the bed and there was fire in her eyes. I could actually see my wife's faith.

Each mountain that the devil had put in front of Cheryl, God has miraculously moved. At 11 years old, her faith brought her through a car crash. She went through the windshield. The engine came in and crushed her leg and crippled her. God put a bone in her left leg where there was no bone. She had a cracked back and God healed her back. She had over a hundred stitches in her face...without having plastic surgery. God healed her face. Her faith said Satan was not going to steal her dream. This little girl sought God many times for healing. Through her faith, courage and determination she became Miss America!

Cheryl told me that when she walked down the runway wearing the coveted crown of Miss America on her head, the thought flashed through her mind, "I would never have received all this if I hadn't chosen to believe that God would heal me. I would still be back in Choctaw County, Mississippi wearing the flour sack dresses my mother had made for me...and walking with a limp for the rest of my life."

As a man, Cheryl's faith was hard for me to take. My wife has stronger faith than I do! I knew where my faith was. I had no faith when I flew to Dallas. I asked myself "Where is your faith, man?" I questioned myself over and over. Satan attacked me with everything he had. He was trying to shake what little faith I had!

Negative thoughts raced through my mind, "Your wife stood alone when she was a little girl. Your wife is standing alone right now. *Man, where is your faith?*" It started working on me. "You work for Oral Roberts, you're surrounded by faith people, that's what you do! You're supposed to have faith."

I knew I was like many men in the ministry. I knew the Word, I breathed the Word, I spoke the Word, I gave the Word to others but I lacked sitting down and saying, "OK, Father God. Let's have a personal relationship. I want to talk to you. I want you to talk to me. At that moment in my life, I felt God saying, "Come closer to me, Harry."

I didn't understand exactly what that meant. I had never had a father-son relationship. My father died when I was very young. Now, I knew without a doubt that the time had come for me to *learn how* to have that kind of relationship...for my sake and the sake of my family. My family needed me to be strong spiritually.

The doctors still told her we had lost the baby and they wouldn't back off that. An hour after the doctor did the examination Cheryl was still bleeding so profusely that they took her to the hospital ultrasound department so they could x-ray her. The ultrasound technician said, "Hmm. There's your right ovary and it has 10 maybe 12 tumors on it. Now let's see...why, there's the baby right there."

Cheryl exploded. "There's our baby! I can see her with my own eyes. I can see her kicking and preaching in there!" She almost fell off the table to get a good look! She started praising God and thanking Him...singing in the Spirit. She was convinced she saw our daughter! (Although at that time we didn't know if it was a girl or a boy!) That was the beginning of Gabrielle. To this day, she talks nonstop!

When she turned the corner on the way back to the emergency room Cheryl saw the doctor. He was at one end of the corridor and she was at the other. She started yelling, "Doctor. Isn't it great? I didn't lose the baby. This baby will live and not die and declare the works of the Lord in his or her life." (Psalm 118:17,18)

The first thing the doctor said to her was, "I don't care what you saw in the ultrasound. There is no hope that this baby will live." We looked at each other and we looked at him and Cheryl said, "It's too late for you to tell us that there is no hope. This baby will live and not die and declare the works of the Lord in his or her life!"

Cheryl talked about her faith to anyone who would listen. The more she spoke the words into existence the stronger her faith grew. Cheryl would say with her eyes flashing, "God and the devil both know when you mean it. And I mean it! The devil knows when you mean it. God knows when you mean it because He knows how strong your faith is. I may be saying the words with my mouth but words are the only thing that transcends the flesh, the spirit, and the soul. Words go into all realms at all times. I can't step off into the supernatural realm where the angels and the demons work and move but I can send my words into that realm at all times."

When we shared our faith with the doctor he said, "Whatever. Take her across the street to the hotel. She will lose the baby tonight. Then take her home. If by some miracle she still has the baby by morning she will need to be on full bed rest for the next seven and a half months." We had to drive home, we couldn't fly.

For seven and a half months we believed God for a miracle. We believed against all hope, against all odds, against everything that we could see and the doctors told us. Cheryl had to lie flat on her back. Up until this time, we hit the road running every morning. You can't imagine what it was like for Cheryl to lie flat on her back unable to get up. She could only get up to go to the bathroom. She had to eat her food in the bed. She had Thanksgiving coming up...the holidays.

Cheryl was "the mother of the year" type of person. She was very self sufficient. She didn't want anyone else doing her job. She had always done her own cleaning. She grew up doing that and she hasn't changed. She wanted to take care of her own children. I jokingly told her it was "like having King Kong caged...trying to get out!"

People would ask her to speak and she would say, "We can just get one of those little stools and prop me up to talk to the ladies." I said, "No. This is our baby and this is important. You don't have to prove anything to God. You don't have to prove anything to the people, you just stay in bed." That tore her up. Cheryl had to learn that she didn't have to win God's approval. She already had it but she didn't know that.

While she was in bed I did everything. I took care of the children. I did the shopping and the cleaning and the coupon cutting. I cooked and cleaned. Through that experience I learned to respect what she did. I respected her as a minister and as a mother and homemaker.

God used this time to talk to both of us. He helped us create a strong bond with each other. Cheryl loved her ministry and though I hadn't wanted it to, it bothered me. As a man, I wanted her to love me as much as she loved her ministry. It was difficult for her because she was having a hard time separating loving her ministry from loving her God.

It took pulling herself away from the ministry and lying flat on her back for seven and a half months to realize that she wasn't in love with her ministry, she was in love with her God. When she made this distinction it made a big difference.

During that time we grew closer and became intimate with each other...each of us revealing things that made us vulnerable to the other. Once we understood each other's perspective it made a difference in our relationship but understanding each other took time, years really, so don't get discouraged.

8

Do What It Takes...Not Just What You Can

When Cheryl became sick and went through eighteen months of depression, I asked myself "What can I do?" My initial thought was, "I'll do what I can...I'll look into it." Then it struck me. *"You can't just do what you can. You have to do what it takes!"* Cheryl would have not just stopped at doing what she would do if the roles were reversed. She would have gone much, much further. She would do whatever it took.

There is a statement that I heard when I was a little boy that I have remembered all of my life. "Do what it takes...not just what you can." When someone asks you to do something for them, you might answer, "Well, I'll see what I can do...or I will do what I can." I'm here to tell you that if I had only "done what I could" there is no telling what might have happened to my wife and children. I knew in my spirit I had to give it everything I had!

At first, I thought it was something that I could just "fix" as I had many other situations in my life. I was like many men, I just wanted to "fix" her illness so we could go on with our lives. I was doing all I could to stop the problem. I thought you could fix the problem by seeing the doctor.

When my little boy broke a toy he would bring it to me to fix. I could usually fix it because it was something physical that I could manipulate. This worked fine when I was dealing with simple, physical things.

I asked myself, "What happens when I need something fixed that is out of my control?" I didn't know how to "fix" something that wasn't something I could see and touch. What made it hard in Cheryl's case was that we weren't sure what was wrong. First, we had to get a grip on what was happening to her. Then go after it with full attention and effort. Deep in my spirit, I knew where to find the answer.

I would have to connect with that Source that Cheryl had when she was a little girl in Choctaw County, Mississippi. I would have to find the God that Cheryl had as she lay in the hospital after her car accident, the God that touched her life as she lay there in the hospital in excruciating pain with a crushed leg. I was going to have to connect to the God that helped her refuse to accept the words of her doctors, friends, and even church people when they told her to accept being crippled for the rest of her life. *Cheryl refused to listen to them.*

Cheryl did what it took! She made a quality decision to believe God. She could have given up and accepted the words of her family, minister, and friends and just settled for the inevitable. Cheryl would not easily accept the injuries that she could see with her eyes. She went to her Bible and searched for answers. She wanted to know if God would heal her. When she found that God healed a man with a lame leg in the Bible she knew that God would heal her leg too.

She addressed the supernatural and got out of the natural. She expanded her beliefs. She looked past those things that she could see and focused on the unseen. *She focused on the things she could not see—the supernatural—and not the things that she could see—in the natural—and God answered her prayers. She received what she could not see.* Cheryl believed in what she couldn't see. She saw her leg whole and healed. She saw herself not as a cripple but as a miracle. As it says in Romans 4:17 she "...called those things which be not as though they were." King James.

My mother was a young woman when my father died. If she had listened to all the people around her—even her minister—she would probably have split the family up. She refused to accept the fact that it would be better to split up three young children and take them away from their mother. She could have taken the easy way out. It was difficult to go against what everyone was telling her. It was lonely. My mother did not stop at doing what she could *she did what it took!*

Determined to do the best for her children, she too poured over scripture seeking God's guidance. She found a scripture that gave her comfort through the tough times. She claimed the promise in Psalms 146:9 *"...He upholds the fatherless and the widow and sets them upright..."* Amplified. She did not look at her circumstances in the natural...she put her trust and belief in the supernatural. Daily, she put her belief into action while she raised three young children by herself. She did what it took to keep her family together and see all her grandchildren born.

When Cheryl got sick, I was working so hard that I handled it the same way I did everything at the office. I went through the motions. I made decisions that were on the surface. I said, "Let me call this doctor. Let me call that doctor. I'll call Oral and he'll pray for you." These were things I could do to "fix it."

It wasn't until I experienced this crisis in my life that I let down the walls I built around myself...and moved closer to God. God said, "I want you, Harry." He wanted me. He had Harry but He didn't have my heart. He wasn't my leader. He told me I didn't have to be this tough guy. I didn't have to be mad at everybody. He said, "I just want you to pull up a chair and slide next to me. Talk to me and I'll talk back to you. Whisper to me and I'll whisper back." He taught me how to care for my family in a way I never had before. This crisis was a turning point in my life...and in Cheryl's life.

For seven years, I had been the Vice President of Operations of the Oral Roberts Association. Remember, I was responsible for over 1000 employees, many departments, and a large budget. I was responsible for operations, television, and did many things in the ministry.

My cellular phone rang constantly. I would start to play golf with friends and the office would beep me 30-35 times in a round of golf it seemed. It got so my friends were enjoying my golf membership...not me. When I couldn't make it on the course they would call me. "Hey, we're having a great time...wish you were here!" That's how involved I was with work!

Cheryl's illness didn't get my true attention until I saw my wife start to waste away before my eyes. I watched her drift away and become emaciated. When she took her blouse off, you could see her ribs protruding. She started wearing turtleneck sweaters to hide the weight loss. I bought her turtleneck sweaters for Christmas...red, yellow, blue, green.

I knew I had to do something to help her...NOW! I wanted to help Cheryl get well, so I stepped down from my position of vice president and took a lesser position. This position made fewer demands on me. This was a very stressful time. In 1987 all of the ministries were under scrutiny because of scandals that had occurred. Many good ministries suffered along with those that were in error. I was handling all of our press releases at that time. The women's rights activists were coming against all the pageants. Then there was the middle east uprising and everybody hated people from the middle east. Here I was a middle eastern man, working for an evangelist, and married to a beauty queen! It was very stressful.

In the beginning it often seemed as if I had nothing to do at my new position because I had worked so hard before. I had to do something... everything was closing in on me...my family...my little girl...not knowing if she would make it through the night. Cheryl's depression was getting worse with each passing day.

So I began to search for ways I could help Cheryl. I planned a trip back to Mississippi to see her family because I thought it might help her get her mind off things. The trip helped temporarily but Cheryl's condition deteriorated more and more when we got back.

Then one day at home, I had a conversation with Cheryl that hit me hard. We were standing at our kitchen counter. Cheryl choked back tears as she told me, "I just want to slip down in the bathtub or walk in the deep end of the pool and go be with Jesus." I looked into her eyes and there was no one home. In that moment, I became ready to handle the problem with all the power I had in me. I said to myself, "OK. That's it. We're going to take this thing on." *I would do what it took...not just what was convenient.* As I stood at the counter, it struck me. Cheryl would do this for me...and I'm going to do this for her! My wife is dying. It was reality in front of my eyes. Cheryl was virtually dying. It never hit me until that point. I didn't even notice it until my wife became seriously ill.

All of a sudden work wasn't important. I began to accompany Cheryl to the doctor. I wanted to make sure I heard the full diagnosis from the doctor. Cheryl didn't always tell me everything the doctor said. Of course, she had to cram everything she needed to tell me from an entire day into a commercial! I went with her to the dentist when her teeth became brittle and began to chip. I got involved with her total health.

I took care of everything from that point. I resolved to *"do whatever it took."* I made sure that Cheryl ate food that would help her get well. I took care of our boys. I took care of Gabrielle. I took care of Cheryl.

I prepared Thanksgiving dinner and I did all the Christmas shopping. She gave me the list. I got mother stuff, sister stuff, children's stuff and I brought it to the house. I felt as if I was accomplishing something important for the first time in my life.

I searched for foods with the highest fat content. It was Fettuccine Alfredo. I'd go to the restaurant and pick up pizza and Fettuccine Alfredo. I'd buy Haagen Dazs ice cream...whatever had a lot of fat in it. Cheryl liked those little filet steaks with bacon wrapped around it that we had gotten at our favorite restaurant. So I found the meat market that provided them to the restaurant. I bought boxes of those steaks. I brought them home and cooked them. Then I sat down and watched her eat. I wanted to make sure she ate the food.

Every Saturday I cut out coupons. I made out the grocery list and did all the grocery shopping. I started to cook for us. I learned different ways to prepare red meat. Cheryl didn't eat red meat very often. I thought she needed more protein. I wanted to get my wife back so I started watching all the cooking shows and found new recipes for high fat food.

Cheryl had bought items for her to eat that were fat-free. (We later had a nutritionist tell us that our brains are 90% fat. Too many fat-free foods can starve your brain.) I'd go to the store and I'd load up on fat filled foods. I bought ice cream with the highest fat content. I'd go down the road and I'd say, "Let's get ice cream." Many times I brought home a banana split for her. I told her, "Cheryl, we have to do this." She was at the point that she would do whatever it took. I also knew that she was so frugal that she would eat it and not waste it if I had already paid for it!

Cheryl was still ministering at this time. She was struggling to access her faith so she could receive her healing. Through the years, God healed her of many illnesses. Cheryl knew that it was important to "walk out her faith." The thing that was different this time was that she had problems "connecting" her faith because she had an imbalance in her brain that was causing her depression. When she was on stage and under the anointing, she was a ball of fire. Then she would come home on Monday morning and she would be a corpse for three days. She was virtually a walking corpse. That's the only way to say it...she was a walking corpse. She drew the drapes. She didn't have the emotional energy to come out of her room. I said, "You can't keep doing this, Cheryl." But she wouldn't give up. She would say, "Well, I'm fine on stage." That's the kind of person she is...she just doesn't give up!

They asked us to do a Valentine's Day show for TBN. Cheryl's voice was raspy. Her voice was so raspy that you just wanted to clear your throat listening to her talk. In fact, her voice had all but disappeared. The muscles on her neck were protruding. She wore a red dress with pearls up the neck to hide the thinness. Then she went to do the 700 Club. She was wearing a navy blue dress. She was about 90 pounds then. Her fingers were all bones just as they show in prison camp photos! All the time, I constantly pumped food into her. She was eating but she wasn't getting any better. She said she felt as if her body was racing inside!

Time passed but Cheryl just wasn't getting any better. Satan attacked our whole family. The first attack came when Cheryl miscarried and we lost our baby. Then there was an attack on Gabrielle. She developed sleep apnea and we almost lost her. Next, I suffered health problems. Then Cheryl came under attack and became ill with depression. Satan struck our whole family!

We made the decision to get alone with God and to use our energies to receive Cheryl's healing. We didn't talk to a lot of people about the illness because we wanted to stay focused on what God was telling us to do. To get healed we needed to focus on healing. Too many times we talk to everyone about our problem when we should talk the answer.

It's easy for me as a man to operate in the natural...to believe in what I see. I learned that *"doing what it took"* meant having a strong belief in God and in the supernatural. I had to learn how to believe in those things I could not see. I needed to believe...and act in the supernatural. I had to hang onto my faith until our miracle came. I had to change my thinking and believing. I had to change my personal walk with God and my personal relationship with Jesus. I found out that my heavenly Father was always right there with me.

I found out that my closest friend in the world was my Heavenly Father. I often pulled up a chair next to Him and talked with Him and knew that He listened.

When Cheryl became ill I was desperate for answers. I began to seek God in a deeper way than I ever had before. I prayed more...and I read and studied my Bible more. There were nights I couldn't sleep and I would go downstairs and pick up my Bible. I had always thought that God had to speak to me in some spectacular way...as He spoke to Moses from the burning bush. But during this terrible time for our family, I learned that God comes to me when I seek Him. Those nights He met me at the point of my need.

One night the Lord asked me, "Are you trying to control Me?" I realized that is exactly what I had been doing. I was telling Him how to do it. What I really needed was to trust God enough to get close to Him. I needed to listen to "that still small voice."

During the months of Cheryl's illness, I read about the Apostle Stephen. He was a brave man. A real man's man. He was just an ordinary guy like me. When God filled him with the Holy Spirit, he was full of power. He wasn't afraid to speak his mind. Stephen actually *saw* God in heaven just before he died when the heavens opened up. When I read about Stephen, I was able to relate to him. He was a man of firm convictions. He stood alone and believed in God! That was what I needed to do.

The more I searched for God, the hungrier I got to know more about Him. Cheryl and I started talking about things I found in the Bible. She would share something out of the Bible and I would read it. God would reveal things to me. I had heard ministers preach the Word for years but *this was entirely different.* The Word started coming alive and I began to receive personal revelations.

God did a powerful work in my life when Cheryl was sick with depression. I had stored up 17 years of teaching and scriptures in my mind and heart and now God was breathing life into His Words. God became more real to me than I had ever experienced. I was as hungry for the Word as I was for food.

I began to see myself as I really was...with no illusions. I could see I had made some mistakes by not becoming spiritually involved with my wife and family. I knew that I needed to become the spiritual head of my family. I also sensed that God was stirring up a new work for our family.

During this time I personally met my Heavenly Father and became so close to Him that it seemed as if He was right there in the room with me. In the Bible it says, "God is more than enough." I know that is true...He helped me *do what it took* to meet the challenges that faced our family.

9

Bury the Ghost

Four weeks after we had our conversation in our kitchen, I traveled to Zambia. While there, we received an invitation to visit the president of Zambia. We went to a copper town in the northern part of Zaire, near Zambia on the continent of Africa. They invited us to go into one of their copper mines when we arrived.

We rode with 20 other men in an elevator down into the bowels of the earth. The ride was endless. When we had reached the bottom of that elevator shaft we transferred to another elevator that would take us the rest of the way down. Again, we descended still further into the earth until we had dropped nearly a mile. Imagine, nearly a mile below the earth's surface!

As the elevator sank beneath the earth, I thought of Cheryl. I missed Cheryl like I never had before. I missed the kids but I missed her. Cheryl and I had become very close through her dependence on me. When I traveled previously I had been able to put the distance between us on a business basis. Now God had opened my heart and made me feel tenderness that

I hadn't experienced since we were first married.

Both Cheryl and I felt the Lord was doing a new thing in our lives. The Lord had shown me a scripture in Isaiah 43:18-19,

> *"Do not (earnestly) remember the former things; neither consider the things of old. Behold, I am doing a new thing! Now it springs forth; do you not perceive and know it and will you not give heed to it?"* Amplified. We needed a new thing in our lives.

Our crew went down into a copper mine and shot footage for the television program. I felt I had to go down there to bury our pain. I remember going down...down...down. An hour and a half later, I was in a hundred degree heat. It was dark. There was sulfur and diesel fumes in the air. I was soaking wet. I have to tell you...I have a bad case of claustrophobia. We passed the little room with dynamite in it. I thought, "What am I doing here?" That dynamite could explode and it would all come down on my head. But somehow my faith said I could go down into that mine...and I did! When we got down to a big dug out level I said, "OK, let's shoot our scene. This is as far as I go!"

In my frame of mind I thought I was in hell. I mean it was just hell...that's all I can say. We were in a little tunnel or cave. We went where no one had gone before. For 45 minutes, we walked behind a huge machine that clawed the earth. They were actually digging right in front of us! We went where no men had ever gone before...no man had walked that path where the huge machine was digging. I couldn't believe that men worked 12 hours a day, 7 days a week down here in this mine!

I was keenly aware that I needed to bury many things from our past. I needed to bury Cheryl's depression and abuse. I needed to bury my pride and my fearful thoughts that came to me saying, "When your son is ten years old you are going to die just like your father. You are going to leave your son fatherless just like you were left fatherless; the generational curse was trying to pass down another generation! I had to stop it and I knew I could and I had a spiritual right!!"

While we walked in this tiny tunnel filled with the fumes of sulfur in 100 degree heat...God brought a scripture, Matthew 8:28, to my mind.

> *"And when He arrived at the other side in the country of the Gadarenes, two men under the control of demons went to meet Him, coming out of the tombs, so fierce and savage that no one was able to pass by that way. And behold, they shrieked and screamed, What have You to do with us, Jesus, Son of God? Have You come to torment us before the appointed time? Now at some distance from there a drove of many hogs was grazing. And the demons begged Him, If You drive us out, send us into the drove of hogs. And he said to them, Begone! So they came out and went into the hogs, and behold, the whole drove rushed down the steep bank into the sea and died in the water....And behold, the whole town went out to meet Jesus; and as soon as they saw Him, they begged Him to depart from their locality." Amplified.*

Now in the deepest part of the earth, miles from the surface, I began to pray, "Father God, as spiritual leader over my wife and children I bury every attack of Satan against my family...everything that has come against our home. I bury Cheryl's depression here beneath the bowels of the earth. I bury the abuse. I bury my pride. I bury my dad's death. I bury my fearful thoughts of leaving my children fatherless. Down here where no man has ever walked before I bury these things. I bury *every* attack of Satan! I bury these attacks and cast them out of my family."

I thought this is the deepest point I'll ever go. These things came from the pit of hell and they had to go back there. I buried all the pain down there! In the Bible, Jesus cast the demons into the swine and drove them over the cliff. The water was a cleansing. My pain left when I finished my prayer. I really *believed* that I was going to have a new wife when I got back home! What I didn't realize was it was the first step in the beginning of a whole new me!

As our elevator began to rise out of the depths of the earth, leaving the tunnel and darkness far below, I breathed a sigh of relief. I knew deep in my heart that our family was free from the attacks on our lives and that I had buried them deep in the earth. The attacks on our lives disappeared just like the animals that Jesus drove over the cliff and drowned in Matthew 8:28.

We stayed in the home of the president of the nation. When we got back to the house I couldn't wait to talk to Cheryl. I finally got a line out and I said, "Cheryl, today, while I was down in a copper mine, I buried all the attacks of Satan on our family." When I told her she wasn't sure what had happened to me. She said, "Are you OK? (And thought to herself how loving I sounded." She knew about my claustrophobia. I told her, "I just believed that the Lord was telling me to bury the depression and all the attacks on our family. I did and I believe He is healing our family." That night I just felt the curse *lift* off my family. I knew there was something new about to happen in our lives!

For the first month after I got back I didn't turn the TV on at night. Cheryl said, "What's wrong?" I told her, "I love you...I want to be with you and talk to you. I broke the pain that was hanging over us."

God did not cause Cheryl's illness but He used that time to teach me things that have changed my life and the lives of my family. He taught me how to be the spiritual leader of my family. During this time, I began to see what it *really means* to care for my family. How important it is for a man to have an intimate relationship with his Father God. I began to see my family the way God saw them.

The things that have eternal value...like loving my wife and teaching my children to walk in the love and admonition of the Lord...is now my number one priority. For years, I focused on 'material things'...things that will pass away. During this crisis, I discovered what is *really* important. *I learned it wasn't things!*

My idea of what it meant to be a good husband and dad was things like putting the food on the table, putting a roof over my family's head...being a provider. I'm here to tell you...I was wrong.

I do everything I can now to teach men that being a good financial provider is not the most important contribution they can make to their family. Most men do not take spiritual leadership over their families. The world teaches them that they are successful if they provide well for their families. I was no exception.

I took the responsibility of taking physical measures to prevent bad things from happening to my wife, our children and our home. I locked the doors at night, turned on the alarm. I researched and shopped for a car that was safe for my family to ride in. I put a fire alarm in the hallway of our home...in our children's bedrooms. I checked out the coach and school system, because the people have a daily influence on the lives of my children. I accompanied my wife to the mall so she would be safe. I had outside lights for evening safety. I was attempting to prevent something bad from happening to my family by providing physical protection. I wanted to protect my family from danger...from the problems of the world.

I continue to make natural, physical provisions for my family as any father and husband should. Now God *helps me* provide for the needs of my family. I seek Him every day asking for physical provisions for my family. He brings financial provision that I would never have thought of by myself. However, that's only part of what my family needs.

God opened my eyes, and for the first time in my life I saw that my earlier refusal to trust God and get close to Him had a spiritual impact on Cheryl and our children. I missed out on a lot not being spiritually connected with them. I had received my salvation but I was always "too busy" to spend time talking with them about the Lord.

I found the courage to get close to my Father God. I pull up my chair and sit close to Him. He is right there in the room with me. I know He loves me. He shows me how to love and care for my family.

I really believed that when I got home from Africa that I was going to have a new wife...and I did. We had a new relationship from that day forward. God began to speak to Cheryl about not seeking God's approval or man's approval and to stop "performing" for God and people. When I began to change before God...so did Cheryl. She began to be "spirit of God" led and not led by the "needs of people." It was the beginning of healing the root cause of depression. Cheryl began to realize that God could use doctors and medicine to help her connect her faith to her miracle.

10

His Secret Hiding Place

Psalm 18

During the worst part of my depression...in my deepest despair...in the darkness of the night...I ran to be in the arms of my Father God.   Sometimes I would weep endlessly...sometimes I would praise Him from deep inside of me. All I could say was, "Lord, I don't even know who I am inside, but *all that is (deepest) within me, must praise Your name." Psalm 103:1 Amplified.*

At one of the lowest times in my life the scripture that helped me understand what was happening to me more than any other was Psalm 18. No one around me was able to describe the way I felt as this Psalm did. God reached down and touched my heart in this revealing Psalm. David's words helped me see that I was not the only one of His servants who had walked through the valley of depression. David...the man after God's own heart...had felt the feelings I was feeling...and knew the pain I knew.

David begins this Psalm by praising God and telling Him

how much he loves Him. The respect that David felt for the Lord shines through.

> *"I love You fervently and devotedly, O Lord, My Strength. The Lord is my Rock, my Fortress, and my Deliverer; my God, my keen and firm Strength in Whom I will trust and take refuge, my Shield, and the Horn of my salvation, my High Tower. I will call upon the Lord, Who is to be praised; so shall I be saved from my enemies."*
> *Amplified.*

Note: David had a deep reverent love for God. He knew that God inhabits the praises of His people. When he talked to God he always told Him how thankful he was for the many blessings that God had bestowed upon him. His praise and love for God were genuine and came from deep within his heart.

David had settled in his mind forever Who his Source was. When he needed refuge or protection, he knew that the only One who could truly protect him was God. God had protected and delivered him many times. I Samuel 17:37 describes God's protection over David. *"The Lord Who delivered me out of the paw of the lion and out of the paw of the bear...."* *Amplified.* David knew where to go for refuge because God saved his very life repeatedly. David didn't question where to go; he knew immediately that he would turn to God.

When I was a little girl, I learned that God was my Source. When my friends and loved ones told me that I would have to accept being crippled... God breathed new life into my leg. Now when I have any problem I always turn to God first...He is my refuge...my deliverer. I know He loves me and cares for me.

> *"The cords or bands of death surrounded me and the streams of ungodliness and the torrents of ruin terrified*

me. The cords of Sheol (the place of the dead) surround-
ed me; the snares of death confronted and came upon me."

Note: During my depression I often felt surrounded by the enemy. I felt what David felt. I felt as if death was upon me and confronting me. I felt as if death was in my face. My disease did not happen all at once. I received one attack after the other from Satan. At first it was the heavy depressed feeling, then weight loss, splitting headaches, and finally the loss of my voice. My faith believed God was healing me but in the natural I sometimes felt overwhelmed when things attacked me in one wave after another. It gave me peace to know that I could focus on God and that He was my hope of rescue in the midst of the storm.

"In my distress (when seemingly closed in) I called upon
*the Lord and cried to my God; **He heard my voice** out of*
His temple (heavenly dwelling place), and my cry came
before Him, into His (very) ears."

Note: One of the most secure things that happens when you have faith in God is that you know without a doubt that God hears you. In the natural, I was still sick and it appeared as though no one heard my prayer. My faith could falter and sometimes God seemed far away but deep down inside I had the confidence that God heard me and that He would answer. Knowing that God heard me helped me maintain my stubborn faith. I trusted that God heard me and would bring me through on the other side. I think the battles we fight here on earth will take on new meaning when we get to heaven and have a better understanding of what was taking place during the time of our struggles.

Job 23:10 describes his great faith in God during his struggle. *"But He knows the way that I take (He has concern for it, appreciates, and pays attention to it). When He has tried me, I shall come forth as refined gold (pure and luminous). Amplified.*

Job was willing to trust that God knew what was happening to him and that He would use it for his greater good in the end. And that's exactly what happened.

> *"Then the earth quaked and rocked, the foundations also of the mountains trembled; they moved and were shaken because He was indignant and angry. There went up smoke from His nostrils; and lightning out of His mouth devoured; coals were kindled by it. He bowed the heavens also and came down; and thick darkness was under His feet. And He rode upon a cherub (a storm) and flew (swiftly); yes, He sped on with the wings of the wind. He made darkness His secret hiding place; as His pavilion (His canopy) round about Him were dark waters and thick clouds of the skies. Out of the brightness before Him there broke forth through His thick clouds hailstones and coals of fire. The Lord also thundered from the heavens, and the Most High uttered His voice, amid hailstones and coals of fire. And He sent out His arrows and scattered them; and He flashed forth lightnings and put them to rout. Then the beds of the sea appeared and the foundations of the world were laid bare at Your rebuke, O Lord, at the blast of the breath of Your nostrils."*

Note: I could feel God's strength in these verses. They reminded me of how mighty God was and how protected I felt to know He was there for me. The victories I claim in my life happened because I knew that God was there and that He was on my side. Because God isn't here physically it is easy to forget His power. If I ever doubt His might I look at His handiwork...the creation of man from dust...the mighty oceans...the mountain peaks...the biggest animal...to the tiniest insect. I have personally seen God's power when His healing touch restored my leg...even though people told me I would have to be a cripple...God healed me. I know that the God I serve is powerful.

"He reached from on high, He took me; He drew me out of many waters. He delivered me from my strong enemy and from those who hated and abhorred me, for they were too strong for me. They confronted and came upon me in the day of my calamity, but the Lord was my stay and my support. He brought me forth also into a large place; He was delivering me because He was pleased with me and delighted in me. The Lord rewarded me according to my righteousness (my conscious integrity and sincerity with Him); according to the cleanness of my hands has He recompensed me. For I have kept the ways of the Lord and have not wickedly departed from my God. For all His ordinances were before me, and I put not away His statutes from me. I was upright before Him and blameless with Him ever (on guard) to keep myself free from my sin and guilt. Therefore has the Lord recompensed me according to my righteousness (my uprightness and right standing with Him); according to the cleanness of my hands in His sight. With the kind and merciful You will show Yourself kind and merciful, with an upright man You will show Yourself upright. With the pure You will show Yourself pure, and with the perverse You will show Yourself contrary."

Note: David tried to live an upright life before the Lord. Yes, there was sin in his life but he always kept short accounts with God. When he knew he had sinned he immediately went before the Lord and asked for forgiveness. In my walk with God I've found that I often fall short of perfection but I ask God to forgive me for the things I have done that are against His laws and will. When I try the best way that I know how to live for God, He gives me a special "covering" and place of protection. Many people who have stepped outside this covering can attest to the fact that the world is no place to be without the love and protection of God.

I claim His protection for my family because I have tried to live my life for the Lord. I am not perfect...only Jesus was perfect...but God knows that my heart is to live according to His statutes and minister to others about His love. When I read these verses during my depression, it helped give me perspective...to remember who I am in the Lord.

"For you deliver an afflicted and humble people but will bring down those with haughty looks. For You cause my lamp to be lighted and to shine; the Lord my God illumines my darkness. For by You I can run through a troop, and by my God I can leap over a wall."

Note: When you are ill with depression there is a darkness that goes with it. I believe that it is because the disease comes from the Prince of Darkness. There were many days when the light actually hurt my eyes. On those days I would go into our bedroom and draw the drapes...I didn't want to be in the light because it was painful. This verse encouraged me...it made me visualize God actually illuminating my darkness. I could see it in my mind and somehow I knew I could make it...with His strength I could run through a troop and leap over a wall.

"As for God, His way is perfect! The word of the Lord is tested and tried; He is a shield to all those who take refuge and put their trust in Him."

Note: If you truly believe that God is your Source, you know that His way is perfect...even if you don't understand it. If you truly trust Him you have to believe that after you have believed God in faith that God's way is perfect. There is a choice in this verse...God will be your shield if you choose to put your trust in Him. There is great comfort in being on the Lord's side.

"For who is God except the Lord? Or who is the Rock save our God. The God who girds me with strength and makes my way perfect? He makes my feet like hinds' feet (able to stand firmly and make progress on the dangerous heights of testing and trouble); He sets me securely upon my high places."

Note: I knew my strength would have to come from the Lord because I didn't have much strength of my own. This verse promised me that God would give me His strength and make my way perfect (even though I couldn't see it at the time). It promised that when I walked through jagged places He would make my feet strong and sure...that even in the most treacherous places His hand was on my life.

"He teaches my hands to war, so that my arms can bend a bow of bronze. You have also given me the shield of Your salvation, and Your right hand has held me up; Your gentleness and condescension have made me great."

Note: I learned early in my life that wishing would not make Satan go away. I had to learn to fight him. Just as David fought a physical enemy, I fought Satan on a spiritual level. I used the weapons of spiritual warfare against him. I had to be thorough and I had to be resolute. Satan had to know that I was serious. That is why I was so stubborn when Harry asked me to take the medicine. I was in the midst of the battle...a battle I had fought many times before. God used Harry to show me that He had chosen the delivery system of medicine to help me get healed. My faith was that prayer alone would heal me...God surprised me when He used prayer and medicine to bring about His miracle.

"You have given plenty of room for my steps under me, that my feet would not slip."

Note: When I fought one of the most difficult battles of my life, there were times that I had the sense of losing my way. I had never had an illness like depression...it was as if I was adrift at sea heading for uncharted land. I wasn't always sure I was making the right decisions. Just knowing that God was my anchor and that He had promised that my feet would not slip helped me remain strong.

> *"I pursued my enemies and overtook them; neither did I turn again till they were consumed. I smote them so that they were not able to rise; they fell wounded under my feet. For You have girded me with strength for the battle."*

Note: There were times that the only strength I had was the strength that came from the Lord. Many times I felt weak from the battle. If God had not upheld me during the battle I would not have made it. What I could see in the natural was all so negative (that's the way it is when we fight Satan) that I needed His strength daily...hourly.

> *"You have subdued under me and caused to bow down those who rose up against me. You have also made my enemies turn their backs to me, that I might cut off those who hate me. They cried (for help) but there was none to deliver-even unto the Lord, but He answered them not. Then I beat them small as the dust before the wind; I emptied them out as the dirt and mire of the streets. You delivered me from the strivings of the people."*

Note: David knew that God was always right there with him in battle. He depended on God turning the tide to victory when he fought his enemies. I too, as His child, know the assurance, that although victory seemed far away, God was turning the victory in my direction. I have watched Him turn the tide so many times. There is always a time element. I always think I will receive my miracle right away but most of the time there is a waiting period when God not only answers my prayers but sends additional blessings as well.

When He healed me of depression He drew my family closer together than we have ever been and birthed a family ministry as well.

"You have delivered me from the strivings of the people; You made me the head of the nations; a people I had not known served me. As soon as they heard of me, they obeyed me; foreigners submitted themselves cringingly and yielded feigned obedience to me. Foreigners lost heart and came trembling out of their caves or strongholds."

Note: David served God while he was still a young boy. God rewarded his faith by giving him great wealth and making him ruler over Israel. David didn't respect and serve God because he wanted something from Him...he did it because he loved Him. I have loved God from the time I was a young girl and God has given me many blessings because He loves me in return as His child. My love for God has never been conditional and I think it is for that reason that God has used me and blessed me. Christians receive a special anointing to do God's work and God richly blesses His children withholding nothing.

"The Lord lives! Blessed be my Rock; and let the God of my salvation be exalted. The God Who avenges me and subdues peoples under me. Who delivers me from my enemies; yes, You lift me up above those who rise up against me; You deliver me from the man of violence."

Note: Satan rose up against my whole family...he attacked all of us. But God faithfully delivered us all. Lil' Harry should have died from the toxicity of a bowel movement while he was still in the womb shortly before he was born. Shortly after I gave birth to Roman he almost suffocated from heavy mucous in his lungs. I almost lost Gabrielle through a miscarriage...and again after I gave birth. Harry developed heart problems and then I became ill with depression. Satan intended to strike a knockout blow to our whole family...to stop us from what we were doing for the Lord. But his attacks didn't work. God delivered us all from the "man of violence." (Satan)

> *"Therefore will I give thanks and extol You, O Lord, among the nations, and sing praises to Your name. Great deliverances and triumphs gives He to His king; and He shows mercy and steadfast love to His anointed, to David and his offspring forever." Psalm 18:1-50, Amplified.*

Note: There were times in my depression that all I could do was sing praises to God...and sing praises that my healing was not far away. God in his mercy and steadfast love honored my actions by touching us all in a more miraculous way than I had ever imagined.

While I was ill with depression I felt as if death was in my face. I felt that Satan was out to destroy everything that God had sown in our family.

John 10:10 warns us,

> *"The thief comes only in order to steal and kill and destroy. I came that they may have and enjoy life, and have it in abundance (to the full, till it overflows). Amplified*

At first, I thought I was the one Satan wanted to destroy but I came to realize that he wanted to destroy our whole family. By taking me out, it would rip our whole family apart. But Satan was unprepared for the defense we put up as an anointed Christian family. When we believed God and His Word, Satan was no match for us!

11

And They That Are Sick
Need A Physician

Luke 5:31

For months, Harry had been begging me to take the medicine that our spirit-filled doctor prescribed. He pleaded with me. "Take the medicine for the sake of our family. Honey, it's just not you that is affected by this. You've got to look at that baby in the crib and you've got to look at our two boys. This is affecting them and we need you back." He would hold up the tiny pill in front of me. "This little pill will help reform the chemical balance that has depleted in your brain. Why won't you take it?" Or he would say, "If you had diabetes and you had to have insulin to live before your healing was manifested, wouldn't you take your insulin until your healing came? Won't you please take this pill knowing that when your healing is manifested you won't have to take it any more?"

Harry took me to four doctors but I still couldn't accept their diagnosis. They said I had a chemical imbalance in my brain because the baby had robbed me of nutrition in my brain. *I didn't know how to fight depression. My spirit man could not function because of its debilitating effect on my mind.*

Harry and the doctors were begging me to take the medication but I refused. I didn't want to mask my symptoms with medication. I was stubborn because I believed my stubborn faith had helped me receive many miracles from God in the past. When I fought off the attacks of Satan it was my determined faith that always brought me through.

I even fought my sister. When we went home for Christmas that year my sister, who is a pharmacist, got in my face with every medical journal she had. She was reading the symptoms and she would say, "Just look at this list. You have every one of these symptoms." My sister got to me as not many people could. She knew that if she made me mad I would forgive her because she was my sister. When she finished talking to me, I was so upset I said to Harry, "Pack us up and take us home!"

But on the ten hour trip back home I thought a lot about what my sister had tried to tell me. Finally, I asked the Lord, "Lord, am I living in denial? Is there really something physically wrong with me. The Lord said, "Yes, you have a physical problem...go to the doctor and take the medicine."

I reflected back on my study of the Bible. In the Old Testament people *habitually* asked God for His direction when they were about to make an important decision and He would tell them exactly what to do. Today, we can forget to ask Him about decisions we have to make in our lives. He has the answers if we ask Him the right questions.

I made the decision to take the medicine but I combined prayer with the medicine to get well. I believed that both were God's healing sources. I had heard Brother Hagin say, "In the name of Jesus I receive no ill affects from this medicine. I take it by faith. I apply my faith to the medicine."

It is very important to apply your faith to the medicine you take. Don't feel condemned by man. In the darkest of nights...man is not there. Man is not going to be there with your answer. Jesus will be there, healing you and restoring what the locusts have stolen. Joel 2:25 says,

> *"And I will restore or replace for you the years that the locust has eaten-the hopping locust, the stripping locust, and the crawling locust, My great army which I sent among you." Amplified.*

What a promise from the Father God! You might ask, "What was wrong with your faith?" Actually, there was nothing wrong with my faith but there was something wrong with my thinking because I was limiting God to the way He wanted to heal me.

Those who say there was something wrong with my faith really do not understand. They do not have the experience I had from which to draw a conclusion. They have not been in the place of depression or they would not say that. My faith was there. God was there with my healing but my "connector", my extension cord, in this case my mind, had a short in it and it was affecting my being able to receive.

God has told me to tell you that there is nothing wrong with your faith if you take medicine. Only the people who have been where you are really understand what you are going through. I believe that's why God told us not to judge each other. I believe He was saying that unless you have walked in someone else's shoes you do not have a clue as to what they are going through.

The Bible teaches in Matthew 7: 1 & 2,

> *"Do not judge and criticize and condemn others, so that you may not be judged and criticized and condemned*

yourselves. For just as you judge and criticize and condemn others, you will be judged and criticized and condemned, and in accordance with the measure you (use to) deal out to others, it will be dealt out again to you." Amplified.

Don't judge others and bring judgment upon yourself.

Don't feel bad about taking medication if you need help. Get a good godly physician that can help you get balanced and then apply the Word of God to that medicine.

Within two weeks of taking the medicine I began to get better. I could speak to that mountain and have faith it would remove! Before I took the medicine I could believe but I couldn't connect my faith.

As Harry puts it, "It seemed like overnight and I had my wife back! Before she took the medication, I didn't know what she would do. Now I could finally see that she was coming back. I could trust my wife again. I could trust her with my children. I could trust her with her own life. I could look into her eyes and say 'There's someone home! I could see that all of a sudden her brain had begun to function.'

"Now, Cheryl was able to pick up her Bible and believe God. Before she had difficulty connecting her faith. Now, full of faith, Cheryl was back! Her faith was activated!

"Cheryl's illness had been in the emotional and mental...soulish realm. The soulish realm houses all of your emotions. The mind is connected to your soul. That's why she needed medicine so she could use her mind to confess her faith. There was nothing wrong with her faith she just couldn't access it.

"Cheryl and I thank God for our spirit-filled doctor. He knew it was going to take more than prayer; it was going to take the medicine. He treated the whole person. Cheryl and

I believe physical healing sometimes happens in an instant...or you can get healed over time. We also believe God put skilled doctors here on earth to help us get healed.

"Some were healed instantly when Jesus prayed; others were healed as they went. They were *wenting*. Cheryl calls it *walking out your healing*. Now we look at the verse in the 23rd Psalm differently; 'Though I walk *through* the valley of the shadow of death I will fear no evil.'

Notice we walk *through* the valley. Yes, we go into the valley of the shadow of death but we keep on going...we go through it—all the way to the other side—we get out! We are *wenting*."

I told Harry over and over how thankful I was to feel like my old self again. Once again God had brought me through the fire. This time He used a different delivery system. I won't ever make the mistake of limiting God's way of healing power again.

Overcoming is victory. If you're the one standing at the end of the war, you've won. You've won if you are still standing and your enemy is defeated...even though you may be beaten up and bloody. Sometimes we forget that. We think we have to come through the battle unscathed to be victorious but that is not so. You may get a bloody nose spiritually and get knocked about but you've still won!

Every time I go through a battle against Satan, God uses this time to teach me more about how He does things. The subject of medicine has been a difficult one for many Christians but God continues to heal in His time and His way. Here are a few of the things I learned.

One of the first things I came to know is that *we cannot limit*

God in the delivery system He chooses to use to heal us.

Spirit-filled doctors have an anointing from God to perform healing. They have spent many hard years preparing to do God's work. They use many miraculous medicines that are actually the raw materials of God's universe...given to us for our well being.

In Luke 5:31 Jesus said, *"It is not those who are healthy who need a physician, but those who are sick."* *Amplified.* Jesus directed us to use physicians. Is this the only way God uses to heal us? No. But it certainly is one way.

There seems to be two ways to think about this subject. One way says that medicine is the "only" way to receive your healing. These are people that don't use their faith and seek God's Word for their healing. There is a quotation that says, "We haven't lost our faith, we've just placed it in physicians." Many people have placed *all* their faith in physicians but this is limiting to God to one way of healing. The Source of all healing is God.

Another way says that we can only receive healing through our faith and prayer. This is people that are seeking God in their lives. This can also be limiting. God wants us to have strong faith. He wants us to use our faith to receive our healing but this is only one delivery system that He uses. We have a powerful combination to receive healing when we combine our faith *and* medication. The bottom line is that God is Sovereign. It is in His time and in His way that we receive from Him. That's why we must have a close intimate relationship with Him, always relying on His leading us to what we are to do.

We must not stop or limit the flow of God's healing power into our sick bodies. God has many ways to heal us. In the Bible there are instances where Jesus used extremely unorthodox methods of healing. John 9:1 relates one of these unorthodox methods.

"As He (Jesus) was walking along, he saw a man blind from birth....Then he spat on the ground and made mud from the spittle and smoothed the mud over the blind man's eyes, and told him 'Go and wash in the Pool of Siloam.' So the man went where he was sent and washed and came back seeing!" Living Bible.

You'll have to admit that Jesus used a strange method to heal this man...but it worked.

I have learned that we should use all of God's methods. God is the Source. God uses prayer and medicine and all other instruments that are available to Him.

When we close the door on one of God's healing systems by not believing that it is sound we are actually dictating to God how we choose for Him to heal us. It is presumptuous for us to believe that we even *know* God's best for our lives. It is also senseless to cut off anything that can bring us health and healing.

12

God's Natural Medicine

I believe that God has given us *another* delivery system for healing...in addition to prayer and medicine. It is the delivery system of nutrition and exercise. God designed our minds and bodies in such a way that they need the proper exercise and nutrition. And He placed the responsibility of caring for our spiritual, physical, and emotional lives with us. When we are inattentive in taking care of ourselves, we can become ill.

We can mistreat our bodies for years without significant health problems but it is like anything else that we abuse...eventually it breaks down. There is a saying, *"If your car breaks down, you can replace it but if your body dies...where will you live?"* These are sobering words but very true. In order to live a happy, energetic life, our health needs to be a high priority for us.

Only when we lose our health do we realize how important it is. We can have great faith, a family that loves us, and all the possessions in the world but if we are sick and depressed, we can't enjoy them. Let me tell you, when I was struck with depression the things around me were much less important in my life. Most of my thoughts were filled with getting well!

Unfortunately, most of the time we ignore our bodies because...except for a few aches and pains...it appears to serve us well. But then we become sick and our bodies *demand to be heard* by making us depressed or by sending us pain signals.

Then, because our spirit lives in our bodies, our bodies can cause us to have spiritual problems as well as physical problems. Doctors will tell you that the mind and the body are one. You cannot impact the mind without impacting the body. We are a spirit that has a mind and lives in a body. Our spirits live in this physical "earth suit" so to speak. When our bodies become sick, we are sometimes unable to use our faith.

Our mind, spirit, and body are God's most miraculous creation. It is difficult for us to fathom just *how miraculous* our bodies are. But in an age where we can duplicate almost anything...no one has been able to duplicate the human body. For years, scientists have tried to reproduce the human mind and body with little success. They have never been able to create the spirit of man. The body is so intricately designed that it defies duplication.

God has given us a wonderful mind, body, and spirit. Psalm 139:13 describes it well.

> *"You made all the delicate, inner parts of my body, and knit them together in my mother's womb. Thank you for making me so wonderfully complex! It is amazing to think about. Your workmanship is marvelous—and how well I know it. You were there while I was being formed in utter seclusion!"* Living Bible.

There are spiritual laws that guide our lives as well as physical and nutritional laws that govern our bodies. We experience pain when we break spiritual...or nutritional laws.

If we fail to practice the spiritual laws God gave us...we will not reap the rewards. For instance, if we don't give, we won't receive the multiplication of our seed sown. If we are careless in the way we treat our bodies, we will reap the pain and depression of a body that does not function well.

Some diseases are definitely from Satan but we can actually "give place to the enemy" (Ephesians 4:27) by taking poor care of our bodies and allowing him to enter our lives through illness. When we have a sound nutrition and exercise program we make it much more difficult to break through our physical defenses. When we have studied our Bible and know the spiritual laws that govern our lives, we are no easy target for Satan. Again, much of what happens to us in our lives is a result of what we do!

Most of us aren't aware of it but there is such a thing as physical depression. Physical depression can come into our lives as a result of poor eating habits and little or no exercise. Constant dieting can take a toll on our health. Not giving our bodies the number of calories that it needs or the proper nutrition it needs can cause depression. Poor eating habits deplete our body and places it in a vulnerable position. Then we go on a diet and rob it of even more nutrients. The final result is that we become depressed...and finally ill.

In their book *Prescription for Nutritional Healing,* James F. Balch, M.D. and Phyllis A. Balch, CNA describe brain function and nutrition. "It has been discovered that *foods greatly influence the brain's behavior. Diet is most often the cause of depression,* related to poor eating habits and constant snacking on junk foods...Fats inhibit the synthesis of neurotransmitters by the brain in that they cause the blood cells to become sticky and to clump together, resulting in poor circulation, especially to the brain."

Our brains must receive the proper nutrition for them to function properly. The food we eat controls the behavior of the brain. Again, most of us don't realize it but our diets are one of the most common causes of depression.

Many of us are walking around with mild (and sometimes severe) cases of depression from malnourishment. However, most of us do not have a severe case of depression. We just continue to function at a lower level and move much slower. If the depression does not become acute, we don't treat it and we go on with our daily activities the best we can. We are the walking depressed.

As many of you read this I'm sure you will recognize symptoms that you have had...the heaviness, fatigue, headaches, insomnia, hopelessness, and many other symptoms. Some of you have even felt so bad that you just don't want to continue living. But it doesn't occur to you that you have a nutritional problem when you have these feelings.

"Depression begins with a disturbance in the part of the brain that governs moods. Most people can handle everyday stresses; their bodies readjust to these pressures. When stress is too great for a person and his adjustment mechanism is unresponsive, depression may be triggered," says James F. Balch, M.D. and Phyllis A Balch, CNC, in their book *Prescription for Nutritional Healing*.

There are other physical causes of depression. Your doctor should check you for hypoglycemia, allergies, hypothyroidism, and malabsorption when you feel depressed.

You can check yourself to discover if you have an *underactive thyroid* by placing a thermometer under your arm, before you get out of bed in the morning, charting your temperature for a week. If your temperature is consistently below 98.6, you are probably hypothyroid. You have an underactive thyroid. Medical doctors who specialize in nutrition believe this is a more accurate way of discovering hypothyroidism than a blood test. They say that hypothyroidism often doesn't show up in a blood test.

You can check to see of you have an allergy through the process of elimination. When you feel that you may be allergic to a certain food, watch the reaction of your body when you eat it. If you have a reaction you are probably allergic and should eliminate it from your diet.

When your body is unable to metabolize simple carbohydrates (junk foods) it can lead to fatigue, dizziness, confusion, headaches, and restlessness. Eating too many simple carbohydrates can cause hypoglycemia. Finally, when the body is no longer able to process sugar properly you get hypoglycemia.

A menu free from white flour and sugar is a good place to start towards having a good diet. Milk products, including cheese, are very difficult for the body to process. Also, consider eliminating fried foods and junk food from your diet.

Eating fresh fruits and vegetables along with whole grains helps keep your body healthy...and happy. You may feel deprived at first but your palette will soon adjust to the different tastes. There are a number of good nutrition books on the market.

Exercise is also important to your body maintenance. If you want to burn fat, you must first mobilize it through exercise. Exercise also aids in the prevention of many diseases. In addition, when you exercise endorphins are released into your system. Endorphins create a sense of well being.

I have studied nutrition and the impact it has on the body for some time now and I know that the effort you put into good body maintenance is well worth the effort.

I Corinthians 6:19 says, "Do you not know that your body is the temple (the very sanctuary) of the Holy Spirit Who lives within you. Whom you have received (as a Gift) from God? You are not your own. You were bought with a price (purchased with a "preciousness and paid for, made his own). So then, honor God and bring glory to Him in your body." Amplified.

God will heal our bodies but it is our job to take care of the wonderful vessel that He has entrusted to us. Many times people get healed, but they don't change their way of living, eating, resting, etc. The anointing can get you healed, delivered, and restored but you can only keep that healing if you stop doing what you were doing that brought the problem on in the first place.

Remember, "I'm sorry" without repentance is empty and wasted. We have to make a lasting lifetime change if we are to walk in health and keep healings that we receive from God.

13

How We Used Our Faith
To Fight Depression

God chose to use the delivery system of medicine to heal me of depression but I combined the medicine I took with my faith. I strongly believe that if I hadn't had faith in God—along with the treatment I received from spirit-filled doctors—I might not have gotten well.

There are certain steps of faith that Harry and I took in this battle that not only helped me receive my healing but the steps we took expanded our faith and changed our lives as well. There are secure beliefs and promises that have pulled us through many storms in our lives. I'm going to list them here because I believe that in any battle you fight you should have habitual things that you do and believe to come through the storm.

1) **Fight the good fight of faith.** I Timothy 6:12 says,

"Fight the good fight of the faith; lay hold of the eternal life to which you were summoned and (for which) you confessed the good confession (of faith) before many witnesses." Amplified

When I was very young, I learned how to fight the good fight of faith...out of necessity.

On May 4, 1968, I was crippled as a result of a tragic car accident. I not only had a crushed leg, but the doctors at Webster County Hospital discovered additional injuries to my back. Eventually, the doctors performed surgery and when I woke up I had an 80 pound cast on my body!

In addition to these devastating injuries, my face was covered with fragments of broken glass from the windshield. When the doctors in the emergency room finished sewing up my face...there were over 100 ugly stitches that remained. Actually, the doctors stopped counting stitches after they reached 100.

I remember holding a mirror up to my face and feeling nauseated when I saw my reflection. The tear-streaked face of the little girl who looked back at me in the mirror was repulsive. Friends had always told me that I was pretty. In fact, our milkman had even predicted that I would grow up and become Miss America. In that moment, it was a distant impossible dream.

I faced a problem. I could accept the fact that I would be a hopeless cripple for the rest of my life...or I could search for another way out of my dilemma. Even as a child, I'd always felt close to God so I instinctively turned to Him for help. I loved our church but no one had ever said a word about people being healed today. I couldn't understand why God would heal the people in the Bible and not heal me too.

During that time, while I was learning about healing, God taught me a lesson that I have never forgotten. (God often teaches us things when we are in crisis situations. He didn't cause my injuries but He knew He had my full attention and that it was a good time to teach me an important truth.) "What you look like on the outside is not nearly as valuable

as what is on the inside." So I decided I would fill up my
inside with the beautiful words I was finding in my Bible and
let God take care of my outside. In I Samuel 16:7 it says,

> *"But the Lord said to Samuel, Look not on his appearance
> or at the height of his stature, for I have rejected him. For
> the Lord sees not as man sees; for man looks on the out-
> ward appearance, but the Lord looks on the heart."*
> Amplified.

When I was still a little girl, I refused to accept the fact that
God wouldn't heal me. I didn't listen to what people were
telling me. I decided to go to the Source. With the faith of a
little child, I asked God to heal me. (As an adult, I have found
that God has a special place in His heart for *His precious little
ones.*) In Matthew 19:14 it says,

> *"But Jesus said, "Let the little children come to me, and
> don't prevent them. For of such is the Kingdom of
> Heaven." Living Bible.*

When I was just a child He paid attention to me. My need
was important to Him. (He listened and helped me.)

Even though I was just a child, I knew that if I accepted my
crippled leg there was no hope. I read the pages of my Bible
and found scriptures that said God did heal the sick. I didn't
have a lot of faith but the Bible said what little faith I did have
was powerful. In Matthew 17:20 it says,

> *"For if you have faith even as small as a tiny mustard seed
> you could say to this mountain, 'Move!' and it would go
> far away. Nothing would be impossible." Living Bible.*

So I made a decision to take the tiny amount of faith I had
and believe that what God said was true. I decided to believe
God...not man. Even though I didn't know anybody that had
been healed by God, I believed that if God would do it for
one person He would do it for me. Acts 10:34 says,

"Most certainly and thoroughly I now perceive and understand that God shows no partiality and is no respecter of persons." Amplified.

The people I knew loved me but they actually tried to discourage me from believing God. There wasn't anyone around me that thought that God healed people today. I had to fight this battle alone.

What is fighting the good fight of faith? It is believing what you know in the supernatural, instead of what you can see in the natural. It is believing what you cannot see with your eyes. God's Word says He will heal you. When you place your eyes on your sick body, and in the natural there isn't a shred of possibility of healing, it takes strength to believe God.

I told my family and friends that God told me He would heal me. I believed it. It said so in the Bible. James 5:15 promises, *"And the prayer that is of faith will save him who is sick, and the Lord will restore him..."* Amplified. I did not write the Bible...God did. I decided to believe all of what He told me in His word...or none of it. Although I couldn't see my healing with my eyes...I knew in my heart the answer was on the way.

Fighting the good fight of faith is **keeping your mouth in line with your belief.** When you are believing God for your healing you do not confess negative things with your mouth.

1) The negative things your mouth says and your ears hear, will weaken your resolve to believe God.

2) Mark 11:23,24 says that we can have what we say. *"Truly I tell you, whoever says to this mountain, Be lifted up and thrown into the sea! and does not doubt at all in his heart but believes that what he says will take place, it will be done for him. For this reason I am telling you,*

whatever you ask for in prayer, believe (trust and be confident) that it is granted to you and you will get it."
Amplified.

This means that we can have the good things that God promises or we can have the destruction and ruin that Satan promises. So what we say with our mouth is extremely important. We have to be stubborn in our belief. We must stubbornly believe God even though we cannot see any sign of results with our eyes. If you aren't stubborn in your faith Satan will use people to talk you out of what you believe.

If you are only casually interested in having God heal you...you are not fighting the good fight of faith. You have to mean it when you believe God to heal you. God knows when you mean it and the devil knows when you mean it. When God knows you mean business, the heavens break open and God sends His messengers to answer your prayers.

One of the most inspiring faith scriptures in the Bible is found in I Kings 18:41.

"And Elijah said to Ahab, Go up, eat and drink, for there is the sound of abundance of rain. So Ahab went up to eat and to drink. And Elijah went up to the top of Carmel; and he bowed himself down upon the earth and put his face between his knees. And said to his servant. Go up now, look toward the sea. And he went up and looked and said, There is nothing. Elijah said, Go again seven times. And at the seventh time the servant said, A cloud as small as a man's hand is arising out of the sea. And Elijah said, Go up, say to Ahab, Hitch your chariot and go down, lest the rain stop you. In a little while, the heavens were black with wind-swept clouds, and there was a great rain. Amplified.

Notice also Elijah's posture. He bowed himself down and

put his face between his knees. He was in the birthing (intercession) position. He was giving birth to his miracle.

Elijah strongly believed what he couldn't see with his eyes. In the natural, there was no rain and no cloud in sight but he told Ahab that "he heard the sound of the abundance of rain." As it says in Romans 4:17, Elijah was "calling those things that be not as though they were." King James. His faith was so strong that he believed that God would bring the rain...and God didn't disappoint him.

When you are just casually interested in receiving your healing there isn't a lot that can be done for you in the spiritual world. James 1:5-8 says,

> *"If any of you is deficient in wisdom, let him ask of the giving God (Who gives) to everyone liberally and ungrudgingly, without reproaching or faultfinding, and it will be given him. Only it must be in faith that he asks with no wavering (no hesitating, no doubting). For the one who wavers (hesitates, doubts) is like the billowing surge out at sea that is blown hither and thither and tossed by the wind. For truly, let not such a person imagine that he will receive anything from the Lord. (For being as he is) a man of two minds (hesitating, dubious, irresolute), (he is) unstable and unreliable and uncertain about everything (he thinks, feels, decides.) Amplified.*

Fighting the good fight of faith is also **knowing the *level of effort* you have to expend to receive your healing.** It takes effort to stay focused on what you know the Bible is telling you, when everything and everyone around you is telling you not to believe God. It takes effort not to believe what Satan is putting in your mind. It takes effort to search the scriptures looking for God's promises. If you put forth only a small effort you may have trouble receiving from God. God wants our commitment.

Fighting the good fight of faith is knowing that **we may not receive the manifestation of our miracle immediately.** God does not cause sickness or any crisis in our lives but He will use it to teach us more about Him. So I know my answer may come quickly or I may need to wait. When I was sick with depression, I had become accustomed to God answering my prayers, I was restless when God didn't answer. I was so sick and miserable with depression that I couldn't understand why it was taking so long. I questioned that I had done something wrong. In the end I found that God's timing is always perfect. He not only healed my body and mind, he brought our family closer than we have ever been and He birthed a family ministry in the process. Harry continued to be a good man but in the process became a "God centered man" also!

God often answers our prayers in the eleventh hour. His timing stretches our faith...and helps us grow into mature Christians. We have to understand something. *God is more interested in us having strong faith than He is in answering our prayers.* He knows that people with strong faith have the ability to get any need met they face in their lives. People with faith do not lie down and let Satan walk all over them. God has given us a lot more power than we realize. He set up the universe for us to get our needs met through our faith.

Once we *learn* how to become an overcomer we can do it every time! God is a good parent and a good (math) teacher. He is not only interested in us finding the right answers. He wants us to know how we got the correct answer so we can get it every time we are faced with a problem.

2) We are not left helpless or hopeless when we face illness or heartbreak...God is right there with us to love us. When Satan attacks our lives, there is a feeling of loneliness...of isolation. We feel that there is no one around to help us...that we have to fight the battle by ourselves. This is why

we must always ask God to help us. God has given us His written Word that He will always be there for us when we seek Him. During this time my Father God taught me a Bible verse. John 14:12,13 says

"I assure you, most solemnly I tell you, if anyone stead-fastly believes in Me, he will himself be able to do the things that I do; and he will do even greater things than these, because I go to the Father. And I will do (I Myself will grant) whatever you ask in My Name (as presenting all that I am), so that the Father may be glorified and extolled in (through) the Son. Amplified.

There are so many encouraging scriptures in the Bible to assure us that God is thinking about us...that He is a helper in the times of our trouble.

Psalms 40:17 *"I am poor and needy, yet **the Lord is thinking about me right now!** O my God, you are my helper." Living Bible.*

Psalms 55:22 *"**Give your burdens to the Lord.** He will carry them. He will not permit the godly to slip or fall."*

Psalms 56:3,4 *"But **when I am afraid, I will put my confidence in you.** Yes, I will trust in the promises of God. And since I am trusting him what can mere man do to me?...You have seen me tossing and turning through the night. You have collected all my tears and preserved them in your bottle! You have recorded every-one in your book. The very day I call for help, the tide of battle turns...the one thing I know is that God is for me." Living Bible.*

Psalms 57:1 *"O God, have pity, for I am trusting you! I will hide beneath the shadow of your wings until this storm is past. I will cry to the God of heaven who does such wonders for me. He will send down help from heaven to save me, because of His love and His faithfulness." Living Bible.*

Hebrews 13: 5 *"For God has said, "I will never, never fail you nor forsake you. That is why we can say without any doubt or fear, 'The Lord is my Helper and I am not afraid...'" Living Bible.*

3) **God has given us many tools to fight our battles.** The biggest tool He has given us is our faith. In Hebrews 11:6 it says,

"You can never please God without faith, without depending on him. Anyone who wants to come to God must believe that there is a God and that He rewards those who sincerely look for Him." Living Bible.

We have what the Bible calls "baby faith" when we first become Christians. That's what I had when I was a little girl. My faith wasn't as strong as it is today. When I went through battle after battle in my life, each time making a decision to believe God, my faith muscle grew strong.

When I first made a decision to believe God, there was a question in my mind as to whether I should believe God or my family and friends. Then God met the needs in my life so well that I no longer questioned whether to believe God. As my faith grew I had other questions. I wondered how long it would take for my miracle to manifest in my life. Because I chose a strong path in my life to believe God, I'll admit that I can grow impatient when my miracle is slow in arriving. I sometimes wonder why it takes so long for God to answer. I have found in my life that I never know how God will answer my prayers. But I know that He will answer.

I was so sick with my depression that I almost missed God. I sincerely believed He would heal me through my faith and prayers (which He did) but I didn't know that He would also use medicine, another delivery system, to heal me.

4) Searching my Bible has been a strong source of strength. God's spirit touches each page in the Bible...each Word is inspired by His direction. I feel as if I am touching God's hand and heart when I read each passage. There is a powerful anointing upon His Word. I feel God's breath of life in each story in the Bible. The Bible is my road map that teaches me how God thinks and also what He promises to do for me. I learned early in life that it is impossible to have faith without reading the Bible. Romans 10:17 says,

> *"So faith comes by hearing (what is told), and what is heard comes by the preaching (of the message that comes from the lips) of Christ (the Messiah Himself).* Amplified.*

There were many times when I read the Bible aloud so my ears could hear the words and they became part of me. There are important passages that I hang my faith on. I memorize these scriptures to strengthen my faith and use them to fight Satan. Psalms 119:11 says, *"Your word have I laid up in my heart that I might not sin against you."* *Amplified.* When the Word is in your heart it will help you not to sin. Fear is sin. Doubt is sin. Unbelief is sin. The Word of God in your heart can help you keep fear, doubt, and unbelief away from you.

Many times in my life I have picked up my Bible full of questions, anxiety, or fear only to have my whole mind and spirit changed just by reading His Word. The Bible is my refuge...my hiding place. It is my place to get alone with God. When I went through the depression I know I could not have made it without God's precious words to guide, strengthen, and encourage me.

There are many tear-stained pages in my Bible where I have come to God to help me through the night. I have fallen asleep from exhaustion with my opened Bible in my lap. There have been times when I needed comfort that I have held the Bible close over my heart just to feel near the Lord.

5) **We always need the help of people who love us.** There is no way I could have made it through the tough times without Harry's love and faith. He tells it this way. "I truly believe that I was for Cheryl like Aaron was for Moses while she was ill. Her mind wouldn't let her faith activate and kick in so she could get healed. When she was out ministering her arms were up but when she was home her arms were down. I had to prop her arms up and hold her up. I needed to be the covering...I needed to be as the roof over a house. I tried but I had so many holes in me that the place was leaking in torrents. But I patched them up.

"I did everything I knew how to do spiritually. I prayed, the children prayed. We put a prayer cover over her. I started changing. I had to get in the spiritual position to help my wife. I started reading Christian articles. I started listening to more Christian TV. I started *turning off the TV* and listened to God more.

"During this terrible time, God brought Cheryl and me closer together. We began to have long talks about the Lord. She had always wanted a partner in the Word. I had resisted because I felt as if she wanted me to do something I didn't feel a real need to do. Cheryl liked to dig through scripture...I wanted surface. She wanted movement...I didn't. Scrape off the top and you've got me down. I was like most men...I needed the top layer removed. I didn't want it shoved down my throat because I didn't want to swallow!!

"Little by little I started coming out of my cocoon. It was a gradual process. I started to let go of old hurts and fears...and I started trusting God. Cheryl got me a new big Bible and it says Daddy Harry on the front of it. I started studying and making notes in it. I started getting revelation out of it. With each word I read, came the realization that I had to be active in believing God for Cheryl's healing.

"I had to be there for Cheryl. I couldn't say to her, 'You have to deal with this...I'm going to take care of the baby. I'm going to take care of the children. This depression is yours to deal with.' I had to be there for her all the way...both physically and spiritually.

"I had to do what it took to take care of my wife and children physically. I had to do what it took to take care of my wife and children spiritually. I had to do what it took for the next generation and the next generation. I knew if I was the one who was ill with depression Cheryl would "do what it took" to see me through!

"As a man this was a very tender spot for me. It was difficult for me to admit that I wasn't where I needed to be when Cheryl needed me. My wife and children are where my treasure is and this is where my heart is. (Matthew 6:21) I became willing to fight for them in every way I could."

"During the depression, Cheryl would often plead with me to help her. She was close to tears and held her head in her hands. 'I have a splitting headache. My head is going to split right open. You've got to get me some help.'

"This was hard for me to take. I'd always been able to take care of things for my family but now I felt helpless. I came before God and said, 'God, I've done good things for the ministry in my life. I have a receipt with you in heaven that I want to pull out. God, I need it now. I need your strength now. I need that touch now. I need from you like I've never needed before. I want my wife healed. I want my family back. It is my heavenly right to say, *It's my time.*"' (Phillipians 4:19)

"I took her to four doctors. We went from specialist to specialist. We found a spirit-filled doctor that was great. His final diagnosis was that she had a chemical imbalance in her brain. A lot of people thought it was postpartum depression but it was more than that. This actually attacked her brain. The doctors prescribed medication.

"Cheryl, full of faith, steadfastly refused to take the medication. She said, 'I'm not going to mask my illness with that pill.' I said, 'This little pill will help replenish the chemical that has been depleted in your brain. Why won't you take it?' I was talking to the faith girl. She told me, 'God has seen me through many times before. I know what to do. Harry, once you find a formula that works you know what to do. You know what to do to get well.'

"Still, because her mind was suppressing her spirit, she did everything she knew to do but nothing was working. The mind is the receiver. The heart is the processor. The heart can process and understand but the mind connects the faith! I pleaded with her to take the medication. 'Take your medicine for the sake of the family. Honey, it's just not you that's affected by this. You've got to look at that baby in the crib. You've got to look at our two boys. This is affecting them and we need you back.' Being there for Cheryl meant telling her what I thought about the situation. Sometimes we don't tell people we love what we think because we don't want to hurt their feelings or disagree with them but when someone you love becomes ill, you have to have the courage to talk plainly to them.

"If they are believing God for healing and the healing has not come...it may be that God wants to use a different delivery system...just as He did for Cheryl."

6) **Jesus understands our pain...He has walked where we walk.** Jesus felt the pain of our humanness. Many people don't understand that Jesus felt the everyday pains of being human...just like you and me. This was part of God's plan for

Jesus to know and intimately understand our pain so He could help us. Jesus endured the pain of all our sins when He was arrested and beaten. He felt humiliation when people in the crowds spat upon Him. What restraint it must have taken to withhold His power to help Himself. Jesus felt the pain that was to come as He carried that heavy wooden cross up the dusty road to Calvary. In His humanness Jesus even cried out to God "My God, My God why have you forsaken me?"

Jesus knew the pain of isolation. He felt the affliction of depression come upon Him like a cloak. He felt the darkness of the hour...but He was willing to endure the pain in order that we might be delivered from sickness and pain. Jesus actually carried our pain on His body when He went to the cross.

When we feel the pain and isolation of illness we can know that Jesus walked where we walk...we are not alone.

7) We don't have to stay in the valley...but we do have to walk through it. With each valley that we walk through...each battle we overcome...we grow closer to God and to heaven. In John 16:33 it says,

> *"I have told you these things, so that in Me you may have (perfect) peace and confidence. In the world you have tribulation and trials and distress and frustration; but be of good cheer (take courage; be confident, certain, undaunted)! For I have overcome the world, (I have deprived it of power to harm you and have conquered it for you.") Amplified.*

A by product of walking through deep valleys is that we are able to learn important spiritual truths...if we focus our attention in the right direction. The human spirit is refined through hardships. Families are brought closer together to fight the battle. Family members reveal spiritual strengths and values to each other that might have remained buried had it not been for the crisis. When we are forced to dig deep within ourselves, we find out what our priorities are and what we really believe in. When we do this we gain much strength from each other.

In Job 23:10, Job declares his faith that God is in charge and will bring him through.

"When He has tried me, I shall come forth as refined gold (pure and luminous). Amplified. In James 1:12, "Blessed (happy, to be envied) is the man who is patient under trial and stands up under temptation, for when he has stood the test and been approved, he will receive (the victor's) crown of life which God has promised to those who love Him." Amplified.

In Psalm 66:10,

"For You, O God, have proved us; You have tried us as silver is tried, refined and purified." Amplified.

While we are walking through each valley God is perfecting us.

"Yes, though I walk through the (deep, sunless) valley of the shadow of death, I will fear or dread no evil, for You are with me; Your rod (to protect) and Your staff (to guide), they comfort me." Amplified.

We don't have to stay in that valley, but sometimes we have to go through it. God has made us victorious so we can come through it to the other side.

8) **We manifest what we are full of.** The time to prepare for a crisis, is *before* the crisis...not in the middle of it. When we need to believe God for healing we must use the scriptures and promises He has given us. If we haven't read the Bible or memorized any of the verses it will be difficult to receive from God. God in His mercy does sometimes heal us without this

knowledge of His Word but He does not expect that we will remain in a state of ignorance. Jesus searched the scriptures and quoted them often to receive from God. When we do not know the Bible, we have a very vague idea of what God has promised us. Many people even have a distorted idea of what God promises to do for them. If we want to understand the plan...we need to read the manual. Many people get healed but can't seem to keep their healing. I believe when we get a revelation that what we put into ourselves—is what we will manifest—we will all be more diligent and disciplined about filling ourselves up with the Word of God.

For out of the *abundance* of the heart the mouth speaks. Luke 6:45 says,

> *"The upright (honorable, intrinsically good) man out of the good treasure (stored) in his heart produces what is upright (honorable and intrinsically good), and the evil man out of the evil storehouse brings forth that which is depraved (wicked and intrinsically evil); for out of the abundance (overflow) of the heart his mouth speaks."* Amplified.

The Lord spoke to me recently and told me that if we would take the Word of God like a multivitamin rather than chemotherapy then we could learn to walk in health. That's pretty plain. Too often we wait until a crisis hits and we mega overdose on the Word of God trying to absorb and understand and process as much as we possibly can get just so we can survive. Then when the crisis is over the Word is laid aside and not thought of again until the next crisis. This is a shame but it describes many of God's people. His best for us is daily growth, daily maturity, daily filling ourselves up with God's Word and then no matter what comes our way, then we manifest what we are full of.

10) Ask strong people for help. I believe if Harry had not made the very important decision to take over, Satan might have killed me. I believe with all my heart that I owe him my life for his intervention. I honestly think I would have died or emotionally been no earthly good to anyone.

Your wife or husband is there to help you, so let them know what is going on in your mind and heart. Ask a close friend or a pastor, skilled in counseling, to help you if you are not married.

Sometimes we, as human beings, find it difficult to ask the people around us for help. We feel embarrassed because we find ourselves in a depressed state. One of the things that we must learn to do is to ask people for what we need from them. People are not mind readers...they will not know unless we tell them.

Many times *we shut down* and suffer in silence when there are people around us who love us and are willing to help. This act of asking others for help requires that we make ourselves vulnerable to people...but this very act can help us form deeper relationships. It is learning to trust.

It is not recommended that you open up to people, friends or family who lack spiritual depth...often they lack the maturity both emotionally and spiritually to be of help and it can make matters worse.

There are many people around you who are ready and willing to help...if you ask them. Ask people to help you if you want to have close friends.

11) **God will move toward you.** My relationship with the Father was not in any jeopardy, but I was so exhausted that I could not get myself up to get to Him. He had to come to me. He moved down to me. My Father God came down to me, and He will come to you, too.

He came to me in my darkness, and in the pit of my despair.

Psalm 18:16 says, *"He reached from on high, He took me; He drew me out of many waters." Amplified.*

You might ask, "Did you lose your faith?" Absolutely not! My faith stood strong and steady, because my spirit was not affected by the depression.

My Father God, reached down to me, and He will reach down to you. Do you feel like you are under the water, and can see the light above the waters, but you can't come up and take a breath? God will reach down under the water, and take you by His Hand, and He will bring you out. He will pull you up and help you take that first breath. You might feel like the depression, the oppression and even the "suicide" that is so big, is too strong for God. You might feel like you cannot possibly fight it anymore. It is a strong enemy...but God is a strong God! Romans 8:31 says,

> *"What then shall we say to (all) this? If God is for us, who (can be) against us? (Who can be our foe, if God is on our side?)" Amplified.*

God will strengthen you and reach right in the midst of the despair, just as He did for Harry and me. He will bring you out of the deep waters. He will set you on high out of the despair, and out of the reach of the enemy—Satan!

You might be sitting in your bathtub as I was, and wanting to put your head under the water. Maybe you're saying, "O Father God, I love you with all my heart, but just let me come be with You because I don't want to live here anymore."

That spirit of depression, spirit of suicide, spirit of oppression, spirit of anorexia or bulimia that has tried to steal, kill and destroy your life is defeated! I want you to know that God is bigger than that! He is stronger than that! And He will bring you out! You do not have to give up!

Don't give up! Don't give up! Don't give up! God can and

will deliver you out of the hand of the enemy, no matter how you feel!

12) God is not moved by your feelings. He is moved by your faith. You overcome your problems because of the "Blood of the Lamb and the word of our testimonies! Remember, Revelations 12:11,

"And they have overcome (conquered) him by means of the blood of the Lamb and by the utterance of their testimony, for they did not love and cling to life even when faced with death (holding their lives cheap till they had to die for their witnessing)." *Amplified.*

Begin to say "I am better today, whether you feel it or not. Just say it! I am better today...not I feel better today. Say "I am the healed of the Lord today." Say "I am better and better in every way, everyday." Say Psalm 107:20

"God sends His word and heals me and rescues me from the pit and destruction." *Amplified.*

These are the words of your testimony that give God something to watch over and perform. Jeremiah 1:12 says,

"Then said the Lord to me, You have seen well, for I am alert and active, watching over My word to perform it." *Amplified.*

Say God's Word over to yourself and don't be moved by your "feelings".

Many of us think that because we feel so bad God will take pity and help us but this is not the way God works. God is moved by His Words and laws that He has spoken into existence. If you do not know His Word you are unable to claim His promises and it is difficult for God to reach you. You will be saved by the "word of your testimony." If you don't know many Bible verses or promises...start with what you do know...and ask God to come to you...He will...even if you only have a tiny baby faith.

13) Refuse to give up. When you want something from God, you have to stick with it until you get it. It doesn't matter how long it takes. When your faith is set in concrete and Satan knows that you mean it...you will receive what you say.

When a child knows that *you mean what you say*, he won't waste his time trying to persuade you to do what he wants. But if he thinks you might give in to him, he will make many attempts to get what he wants.

It is much the same in the spiritual realm. If Satan knows that you refuse to give up...that you have made a strong, concrete decision to receive from God, he won't waste as much of his time. If he knows that you absolutely refuse to give up...no matter how long it takes...no matter what obstacles you face...he won't stick around as long.

God intends for us to see His Word as *facts* not *suggestions*. Many people are not convinced in the most inner part of their being that God's Word is a fact or law. They start out on their faith journey believing God but when they don't see any changes with their eyes and they wait for a long period of time, they think that God's Word is not for them, and they give up.

The mistake lies in not having a firm resolve...a faith set in concrete...that withstands the storms and assaults that come against it.

When you are sick, seek the help of a spirit-filled doctor if you need to. Don't let what other people might think of you affect your decisions. That's pride. A spirit-filled doctor is part of God's healing team. Then add your strong faith to the doctor's treatment to receive your healing as I did. Then refuse to give up...not matter what it looks like in the natural.

14) Pride can get in the way of receiving from God. As

the Lord helped me receive my healing from depression, he taught me an unexpected lesson. He taught me the role that pride played in healing. Pride is part of the human nature. Pride is also a cause of failure! God began to show me that I needed to humble myself before Him, and that I needed to allow Him to be my Father God once again.

There is a little bit of pride that can get mixed up with faith. I certainly had a big dose of it. The Lord spoke to my heart and said, "Cheryl, this is what is wrong with you, and yes, you can be healed." You see, I didn't get well because I was stubborn. I was too prideful.

Harry has always said that faith is a journey. Faith is what you hold onto until you receive your miracle, and pride is the obstacle between faith and receiving.

My Father God was showing me how Satan uses pride against good godly people. What some people think is humility, is often pride. In my case, not taking the medicine when it was needed, was plain old, "spiritual pride." It was an attitude of "I can do it myself"—and THAT is pride! In the faith walk, when "I" becomes more powerful than God, be careful. This is an indication that pride has taken over your, so called, "faith."

I had crossed over to pride. I don't know when it happened or how it happened, but I know it happened. God showed me the root of pride, and what grows out of it. What comes out of pride is nothing but blame, shame, destruction, and disease.

I did not want any of that in my life! I wanted all the good things from God. That meant saying, "Lord, whatever it takes to get me well, that's what I want." It humbled me into submitting myself to God, including taking medicine—if that was what it took to be obedient to Him. I felt like Peter, in Acts 10:14 & 15,

"But Peter said, No, by no means, Lord: for I have never eaten anything that is common and unhallowed or (ceremonially) unclean. And the voice came to him again a second time, What God has cleansed and pronounced clean, do not you defile and profane by regarding and calling common and unhallowed or unclean." Amplified.

15) Focus on what God says. Through all of this, God divinely intervened, and taught us many things. He taught us not to focus on what other people think or feel. I had to focus on God's Word and on getting well. We had to remove ourselves from people who did not understand what we were experiencing.

In Luke 8:51, it says,

"And when He came to the house, He permitted no one to enter with Him except Peter and John and James, and the girl's father and mother." Amplified.

Some of the people were well meaning, kind, loving people, but if they did not understand what we were experiencing they could not help us.

For instance, if you are lost and need directions, the person giving you directions can't begin unless they know where you are located...where you are and where you want to go.

When Jairus' daughter needed to be healed, Jesus surrounded her with a body of believers who were in agreement with Him. Jesus threw all the mourners out. He threw all the naysayers, and dream-stealers out!

Mark 5:35 describes the scene:

"While He was still speaking, there came some from the ruler's house, who said (to Jairus), Your daughter has died. Why bother and distress the Teacher any further?

Overhearing but ignoring what they said, Jesus said to the ruler of the synagogue, Don't be seized with alarm and struck with fear; only keep on believing.

*And **He permitted no one to accompany Him except Peter and James and John the brothers of James.** When they arrived at the house of the ruler of the synagogue, He looked (carefully and with understanding) at (the) tumult and the people weeping and wailing loudly.*

And when He had gone in, He said to them, Why do you make an uproar and weep? The little girl is not dead but is sleeping.

And they laughed and jeered at Him. But He put them all out, and, taking the child's father and mother and those who were with Him, He went in where the little girl was lying.

Gripping her (firmly) by the hand, He said to her Talitha cumi—which translated is, Little girl, I say to you, arise (from the sleep of death)!

And instantly the girl got up and started walking around—for she was twelve years old. And they were utterly astonished and overcome with amazement.

And He strictly commanded and warned them that no one should know this, and He (expressly) told them to give her (something) to eat." Amplified.

So, Harry and I removed ourselves from those who condemned what we believed or our method of getting well. And there were many. We left them standing at the door, and did not allow them in while we believed for our miracle.

Harry and I knew that we had to get alone with God...and with the people who understood and were in agreement with us. We were focused when we activated this principle. We were able to get diligent before God in this matter of life and death.

Mark 5:35-43 is so clear on this. Jesus was going to Jarius' house to heal his daughter when the lady with the issue of blood came up to Him. She touched the hem of Jesus' garment. This stopped the whole procession toward the home of Jarius. While Jesus was communicating with the woman who was healed, someone came and told Jairus not to bother Jesus because his daughter had died. Jesus heard the man tell Jairus this news, and as Jesus turned to Jairus (I believe He put his hand over Jairus' mouth just as he was about to confess that his daughter had died) and Jesus said, "Only believe."

In other words, I believe that Jesus was saying, "Stop that negative talk-just stop it and believe! You asked...now believe." No matter what it looks like, no matter how long it takes! Say out loud, "I receive what I have asked for. I'm still moving toward my victory. I will keep believing."

16) Don't stay in bondage to secrets. You don't have to stay in bondage to secrets anymore. You don't have to live in lies. You don't have to stay in darkness. You don't have to be blinded anymore! As we proclaim this to people, at first they seem to be shocked, but greatly relieved.

I have learned that Satan wants to use secrets, lies, and darkness to hold us captive. He wants us all to stay in bondage, and he does not want us to be free.

Isaiah 58:6 declares,

> *"Rather is not this the fast that I have chosen; to loose the bonds of wickedness; to undo the bands of the yoke, to let the oppressed go free, and that you break every (enslaving) yoke?" Amplified.*

Praise the Mighty Name of Jesus! I pronounce you free from all yokes of oppression, from all enslaving and tormenting patterns of living! The precious Blood of Jesus destroys all bondage to lies, secrets, and darkness.

Sometimes people are confused and think keeping secrets is the best way. What they don't understand is that Satan keeps us locked up, and in bondage, when we stay in secrets, lies, and darkness.

Remember, in darkness we are ignorant of the light. Even in the natural when you walk in a dark room, your head is down so you don't trip or fall. Turn on a light, and what happens? Immediately you are able to see straight as you are now in the light. You now walk confidently because of the light, and you know you will not stumble.

It can make you sick and hold you captive when you live in the darkness and believe the lies of Satan. Lies can make you a prisoner. When you believe the "lies" it might as well be truth to your life. When you believe a lie, you are going to activate that lie in your belief system. You cannot believe the lies of the enemy! Lies will become truth to you and take you captive.

Darkness is what depression felt like to me. Sunlight or any kind of light was painful to me. During those months I lived in darkness by closing the drapes and shutting the lights off...that's how I lived. It seemed safer to be in the darkness. That was a lie from the enemy! God brings us out of the darkness into His marvelous light! I Peter 2:9 says,

> *"But you are a chosen race, a royal priesthood, a dedicated nation, (God's) own purchased special people, that you may set forth the wonderful deeds and display the virtues and perfections of Him Who called you out of darkness into His marvelous light." Amplified.*

Recent scientific studies report that sunlight helps depression. Natural sunlight has certain vitamins in it that helps depression. Light is life, but darkness kills. God calls us out of secrets, lies and darkness; into His marvelous light!

14

When You Feel Lost and God Seems Nowhere to Be Found...Do What You Know to Do!

God is truly a good God. He has delivered me from another deep, dark valley, and He has taught me things that I can share with other people who are suffering as I did. One of the things He taught me, after I finally questioned Him, was profound and yet so simple.

In the midst of trying to believe God and do what He told me to do I said to Him, "Father God, I am doing what I know to do. Don't You have something else? I need a revelation from You, God." He simply said, "Do what you know to do."

I said, "God, I have not doubted and my faith has not waned. I am doing what I know to do!" Again He said, "Do what you know to do." So I thought, okay, what do I know to do?

I know to pray. I know to read God's Word. I know how to spend time with God and in the Word. I know how to believe, to confess, to receive. "Father God, how long is this going to take?" I asked. He told me exactly what I have ministered to people for so many years..."Until you get it."

"Until you get it." It seems as if my life has been nothing but proof of that word! "Until you get it. Until it is manifested."

My life is a living example of that word. I was crippled for six years from the car wreck, had over one hundred and fifty stitches in my face from more than one windshield. I lost pageants for five years before becoming Miss America. I was sexually abused ten years, and 20 years went by before I was completely healed of the abuse. How long? Until I got it!

I continued to do what I knew to do. At this point a light broke through my depression. God enlightened my darkness as I mixed my faith with what I knew to do.

Let me encourage you to just continue to do what you know to do. If you don't know what to do then go back and do what I did. Seek God's presence, His Word, His Faith...learn how to walk in His presence.

Another thing that I did was pull out all my old Bibles. Remember the Bible you had when you were first saved? Remember the Bible you had when you were first filled with the Holy Spirit? Everything that you heard you wrote down in the margins of your Bible. I change my Bible every one to two years, so I had a lot of Bibles to read through.

God told me to read the margins of my Bibles and get all the nuggets that His people had put into me. I got hungry again to hear God's revelations. Each day I would pull out another old Bible. Each day these revelations brought a little more light.

I began to realize that I had gotten comfortable in my faith. I needed a booster shot! God said, "Go back to the foundation and rebuild it." It took discipline and time but I did it!

These were the steps of "doing what I needed to do." I read through the New Testament over and over each time writing down God's direction. I remember the first time God told me to do this. He instructed me to write out every scripture pertaining to healing and leave a blank for my own name. Wow! What a job. There were hundreds of scriptures-and many notebook pages of healing scriptures with my name in there—by the time I got through the book of Revelation.

God showed me that somewhere along the line; I got too busy. I got so busy doing God's work that I didn't spend the kind of time with God that I had before. I got so busy developing relationships with the whole world that I forgot my covering. I was busy protecting my family, protecting my ministry, protecting my friends, and protecting everyone else. I forgot to pray for me. I was not covering myself as God's woman of the household, and as God's woman of the calling. I was busy with God's busy-ness. God told me that it was a privilege for me to serve Him. He did not mean for it to be slavery! He told me that He was not impressed with my busy-ness for Him.

I had always covered myself with Psalm 91, which had come alive to me after I was filled with the Holy Spirit. The words of this beautiful Psalm had walked out of the pages of the Bible and into my heart. They were so exciting to me. I let Psalm 91 flow out of me. Then when I married Harry, I would pray Psalm 91 over Harry, then Lil' Harry III, then Roman, and then Gabrielle.

God showed me that somewhere along the way that I got so busy praying for everyone else; I wasn't praying Psalm 91 over me! God took me right back to 23 years ago. He took me back when I was first spirit filled and He helped me remember how exciting and fun it was to be in His presence. I got back into Psalm 91 and developed a sermon just for myself. I titled my sermon to myself, "How to get out of the mess you are in!"

Psalm 91

"He who dwells in the secret place of the Most High shall remain stable and fixed under the shadow of the Almighty (Whose power no foe can withstand). I will say of the Lord, He is my Refuge and my Fortress, my God; on Him I lean and rely, and in Him I (confidently) trust! For then He will deliver you from the snare of the fowler and from the deadly pestilence. (Then) He will cover you with His pinions, and under His wings shall you trust and find refuge; His truth and His faithfulness are a shield and a buckler. You shall not be afraid of the terror of the night, nor of the arrow (evil plots and slanders of the wicked) that flies by day. Nor of the pestilence that stalks in darkness, nor of the destruction and sudden death that surprise and lay waste at noonday. A thousand may fall at your side, and ten thousand at your right hand, but it shall not come near you. Only a spectator shall you be (yourself inaccessible in the secret place of the Most High) as you witness the reward of the wicked. Because you have made the Lord your refuge, and the Most High your dwelling place. There shall no evil befall you, nor any plague or calamity come near your tent. For He will give His angels charge over you to accompany and defend and preserve you in all your ways (of obedience and service.). They shall bear you up on their hands, lest you dash your foot against a stone. You shall tread upon the lion and adder; the young lion and the serpent shall you trample underfoot. Because he has set his love upon Me, therefore will I deliver him; I will set him on high, because he knows and understands My name has a per-

sonal knowledge of My mercy, love, and kindness—trusts and relies on Me, knowing I will never forsake him, no never! He shall call upon Me, and I will answer him; I will be with him in trouble, I will deliver him and honor him. With long life will I satisfy him and show him My salvation." Amplified.

Once again, God brought me back to these beautiful verses. Verse one tells us something so simple...we must get in a secret place. Psalm 91:1 promises,

"He who dwells in the secret place of the Most High shall remain stable and fixed under the shadow of the Almighty (whose power no foe can withstand)." Psalm 91:1 Amplified.

God told me to go to that secret place...and stay there. He told me that many of His people come for a visit and pass through but they do not stay there. He told me His secret place is not a Holiday Inn but a *dwelling place.* When I am in my secret place, it is a secret place away from my enemy. It took discipline to stay in that secret place. I had to make a choice with my will to go into that secret place. God is not going to supernaturally move us into the secret place. We must choose to get there and choose to stay there. God's promises flow when we go into the secret place. We must first do our part...then God's promises follow. Psalm 91:2 says,

"I will say of the Lord, He is my Refuge and my Fortress, my God; on Him I lean and rely, and in Him I (confidently) trust." Amplified.

It is important to make positive God-filled confessions about your relationship with your Father God. Make confessions about your faith. What comes out of your mouth is very important to the outcome of your life. The confessions you make with your mouth...good or bad...create reality.

I have always taught that God is an "if, then" God. God will do His part, if you do your part. God will cover you. He will strengthen you. You will not be snared. Psalm 91:3 says,

> *"For (then) He will deliver you from the snare of the fowler and from the deadly pestilence." In verse four it says, "...His truth and His faithfulness are a shield and a buckler."* Amplified.

You will be protected. God always does His part...after we do ours! If we dwell in the secret place THEN GOD will...Psalm 91:6 says,

> *"You shall not be afraid of the terror of the night..."* Amplified.

No matter what happens you do not have to be afraid. All around you people might give up, but not you. It's too soon to give up. Don't give up! Don't give up! Don't give up!

No matter how the whole world sees you...God knows what you really look like. It doesn't matter what you say to people...God knows the sound of your voice. It doesn't matter how you think the world perceives you...God knows your heart...He knows who you really are.

I have chosen to serve God no matter what circumstances I faced in my life. I made a decision to serve the Lord even when it was not convenient for me to do so. Psalm 91:9-12 speaks about our circumstances. I choose to serve God in spite of my circumstances and situations. Because of my decision "no evil will befall me." I choose to serve God even while circumstances and situations are exploding around me! This is my faith in action.

Psalm 91:13 tells me that I can choose to walk on Satan's head. I can get in his face with the Word of God, the name of Jesus, the blood of the Lamb and the word of my testimony. Revelations 12:11 says,

"And they have overcome (conquered) him by means of the blood of the Lamb and by the utterance of their testimony, for they did not love and cling to life even when faced with death (holding their lives cheap till they had to die for their witnessing)." Amplified.

I have the power to walk all over him.

Psalm 91:14 promises,

"Because he has set his love upon Me, therefore I will deliver him..." Amplfied.

God's promises are meant for His children. In my life I have rehearsed them over and over. God's promises are to deliver me...to set me on high...to answer me...to give me long life...and to show me the way of salvation. God always shows me His way out...not mine.

God is saying to us to choose to get well, be well, and stay well. Through the whole process of being healed of clinical and chemical depression, God never let me forget that "I am somebody to Him." Satan will come in and when he's got you down, he will kick you and keep you in bondage...keeping you captive. But God tells us to choose to get away from the bondage...to choose to get out from under Satan's control...to choose to get well!

Depressions, addictions, abuse, anger, and many other spirits are sent by the enemy to bring us down. But God tells us to "Give them all to me." All it takes is for us to say, "I want to give it all to You right now. I want all my secret areas healed. I want to be healed. I want them all out in the light and out of the darkness. I pray You will set me free from the onslaught of the enemy that has attacked me so many times. In Jesus Name, I believe that I am free, delivered, healed, and whole."

During my depression, I discovered that I had always tried

to be what I thought everybody wanted me to be. I tried to be everything I thought I NEEDED to be. But I found out I am free to be me. Who I am is all God wants. God loves me just the way I am. I've quit performing and seeking approval. I've started living. I was bound by three satanic spirits...a spirit of performance, a spirit of approval, and a spirit of perfection. A threefold cord is not quickly broken as the Bible tells us in Ecclesiastes 4:12,

> *"And though a man might prevail against him who is alone, two will withstand him. A threefold cord is not quickly broken." Amplified.*

But once the Word of God gets hold of it, it must bow its ugly knee to Jesus. All three spirits are broken and I am free! I am healed. I am no longer driven—*now I am led!!*

I didn't like walking through the fierce fire of depression. It was a deep valley. I thought I would never have to walk through such a terrible valley...but I did. But I would walk through that valley a thousand times over to have the relationship with the Lord that I have right now. I have a different assurance. I have a different peace than I have ever had before.

Now I walk on the side of victory. Praise the Mighty Name of Jesus! I am healed from the depression and it sure is nice walking on the healing side of life!

God has healed me, delivered me, and restored me once again and I give Him all the glory. I lift up the precious Holy Name of Jesus, my Savior, and my Deliverer!!

15

A New Day...A New Ministry

When Cheryl was finally healed of depression we discovered that we weren't the same family that we had been before the attack. God didn't cause the illness but He used it in a mighty way to do a deep work in our family. We had been through a trial of fire...one that could have consumed our whole family. The choices we made during that time were the choices of a family that is dedicated to love and serve God. You just can't go through a difficult time like this...where you have been close to God and His love...without it having a deep impact on your life.

After I took on the responsibilities that my wife had carried for years, I gained a new appreciation for her. I had no idea what she did for our family. If you want to appreciate your wife do what she does for two weeks. You'll not only stop and say "I love you." You'll fall in love with her. Before our crisis I loved my wife, now I am *in love* with her.

Cheryl and I knew deep in our hearts that God wanted us to share the things He had shown us with hurting people everywhere. We couldn't explain it but we just *knew* that God wanted us to touch people that only we could touch.

Because we victoriously came through this fire our Father God is opening doors for us to minister...and we are walking on the path that our Father God has prepared for us all along. We know that they are special doors that He has chosen for us because we have experienced first hand what people everywhere face. Ephesians 2:10 tells us,

> *"For we are God's (own) handiwork (His workmanship), recreated in Christ Jesus, (born anew) that we may do those good works which God predestined (planned beforehand) for us (taking paths which He prepared ahead of time), that we should walk in them (living the good life which He prearranged and made ready for us to live)."* Amplified.

For over 18 years Cheryl has been a faithful servant traveling all over the nation ministering and I have been faithfully fulfilling God's call on my life during this time also. We both had totally committed our lives to full time ministry before we married. After our marriage we continued to minister separately...determined to obey the callings God placed on our lives.

We were still trying to decide just exactly what God had in mind for us when we attended a service in Hawaii. While we sat in the service the pastor gave a word of prophecy over me. He prophesied that I would be going before kings, before presidents and that I would be standing in the pulpit. I had never talked to this man before in my life. It was amazing...he was speaking out everything that God had shown us about our new ministry.

Instantly, I realized that we were beginning to enter into a great and powerful move of God. Revelations 21:5 tells us,

> *"And He who is seated on the throne said, See! I make*

all things new. Also He said, Record this, for these sayings are faithful (accurate, incorruptible, and trustworthy) and true (genuine)." Amplified.

God definitely began a new work in our lives when I buried the ghost of our past in Africa. When I was deep within the copper mine I prayed, "Father God, I bury these things and cast them out of my family. Right now we are going forward with the ministry You are calling us into. I receive the new calling on our lives. We will travel together as a family to be faithful and true to our destiny."

We believe God moved us into a family ministry because we understand the attacks on the family by the enemy. We are called to stand in the gap for mothers, fathers, and children of all ages. We have learned that desperate situations require daring faith. Through our faith we are empowered by our Father God to reach the hurting, the broken, the bruised, the abused, and those crushed by the calamities of life.

We have walked through the fire together and come out victorious! We learned that there is great power in agreement and oneness in marriage. We have learned that God's direction for our lives is infinitely more important than anything else.

Satan tried to steal, kill, and destroy our lives and our ministry. He devised schemes to destroy my beautiful wife and our whole family. But through the mighty power of our Lord Jesus Christ we are living miracles!

Cheryl and I have always said that God can take any mess or circumstance that Satan brings into a believer's life and turn it around for His glory. And that is what He did in our lives. We give glory and honor to His Holy Name.

Although the warfare that we have experienced has been strong, our family serves a stronger God! The first great work

God did was to draw me closer to my wife and family. Before the attacks I was only giving my wife a tenth of my time.

For 18 years I have worked all over the world for the Oral Roberts Ministry in crusades. I have been Vice-president of Operations and of television. I believe God used my hard work and dedication in helping a world-wide ministry survive and reach thousands of people. That was the ministry that I performed all those years. Now God is using me to minister directly to hurting people.

In the past, I have been a speaker in chapel but I was not a participator in my own family! I was a great provider but I was not a participator. Without question, I was a good husband and father providing the material necessities of life for my family. I provided food for our table, clothes for our family, and a home to live in. I made certain I provided for my family.

Prior to her illness Cheryl put the covering over our home. She was responsible for prayer. She took the children to church. As long as I put a roof over their heads, food on the table, clothes on their back...I was the perfect provider. I was a good father...but I wasn't a dad because I didn't take spiritual authority and put a covering over our home. Until Cheryl became ill, I had not *wanted* to be the spiritual head of our family. Now I had the motivation to *be there* spiritually for my family.

As Cheryl puts it, "I had always wanted and needed an agreement partner...someone I could trust. It's one thing to have a person say they agree but if you don't have any faith in their agreement you might as well not have agreed with them. Harry began to rise up and become the covering that I needed. He became the agreement partner that I could trust to believe God. When we came into agreement according to Isaiah 54:17, *"No weapon formed against us was going to prosper."* Amplified.

For many years, I was not participating in the spiritual realm at all. Cheryl taught the children to pray, sing, and spent countless hours instructing them in the ways of the Lord. I was content to let her do that. It was fine with me to allow her to be the spiritual covering for our family...but I was wrong!

Cheryl used to say, "Harry, you just need a personal relationship with God." I would say, "I'm trying, I'm trying." She would say, "God isn't going to talk to you through a newspaper or the TV."

God answered Cheryl's prayers. I realized that He had wanted me to slip over next to Him so He could talk to me. For years, I didn't listen. So not only did I get closer to my wife, I got closer to God.

I hadn't realized that as a man there was something lacking in my life. It was hard for me as a man to say "I love you." I thought I had to have this tough exterior. I thought the words "I love you" would make me vulnerable. *God taught me that these are the greatest words in the world.* It's not a loss of your manhood. It is taking the rightful authority that you have to say that you love your family.

It's a necessity for men to put the covering over their home for protection. If we don't place a covering over our families it leaves them wide open to the attacks of the devil. Don't let go of the rope for your loved ones...you may be the only one holding onto that rope.

During the darkest time in my life God taught me a profound spiritual truth...the role of a man is putting a spiritual covering over his family. This is the best way to protect your family. He gave me the desire to participate with my wife and children in spiritual things instead of just being a provider.

God gave me a scripture that clearly illustrated what He

wanted me to do. Exodus 17:11-13 says,

> *"When Moses held up his hand, Israel prevailed; and when he lowered his hand, Amalek prevailed. But Moses hands were heavy and grew weary. So (the other) men took a stone and put it under him and he sat on it. Then Aaron and Hur held up his hands, one on one side and one on the other side so his hands were steady until the going down of the sun. And Joshua mowed down and disabled Amalek and his people with the sword."* Amplified.

This scripture helped me realize that I was the one that was supposed to be the spiritual covering over my family. I took my position by saying to Cheryl, "It's my turn to hold up your arms. I am responsible to not only be your provider, but to be your spiritual leader! I am your husband and we are one."

I refused to say, as I had in the past that "I will let you pray and fight all the spiritual warfare for our home." No! I am taking my rightful place as spiritual leader of our home.

Getting off the sofa and becoming the spiritual covering for my family disrupted my comfort zone! There are many men who are like I was...they need to get off the sofa and put down the remote control!

God desires men to be leaders of their families, not only spiritually but emotionally, mentally, and physically. I encourage men to take authority of their family. Don't run from the responsibility. Embrace your position.

God has given us this awesome leadership role. If our wives hurt, we hurt. We should be willing to say, "I'll walk through this with you, no matter what it takes. I am here for you and we will see this thing through together."

In the past, wives have often had painful experiences

before we knew them. These deep wounds need to be healed and we need to say to our wives, "I was not there, but I am here now to walk through this experience of healing with you."

Men should never say, "That's your problem...you need to go and get help. I do not want to talk about it!" Or "Here's the money...go get help." I have learned that we are one and together as one we will overcome the attack.

Emotional involvement is very meaningful to women. Men see emotional involvement very differently. I know how difficult it is because I am Lebanese. I didn't cry! But I am committed to being emotionally involved with my wife.

The Bible instructs men in Ephesians 5:25,

"Husbands, love your wives, as Christ loved the church and gave Himself up for her." Amplified.

My total participation in every area of my family brings honor and glory to God.

When I accepted my position as spiritual leader of the home God moved us into full time ministry as a family. We now have a new thing with our ministry together. Isaiah 43:18-19 says,

"Do not (earnestly) remember the former things; neither consider the things of old. Behold, I am doing a new thing! Now it springs forth; do you not perceive and know it and will you not give heed to it? I will even make a way in the wilderness and rivers in the desert." Amplified.

One thing Cheryl and I have always said: If someone brought a package to your door and it was a box of rattle snakes would you sign for it? No, you wouldn't! You would say, "Take that back, I did not order that, and I don't want it!" Yet, so many people sign their names in agreement by words or actions and make a covenant with the wrong thing for their lives.

We understand these attacks and we understand the process to be free from them. We have experienced the awesome power of God to bring victory to every situation and to any kind of mess.

Now, we have a new thing. We have our children as part of the ministry. Our wonderful children desire to minister with us. Each is empowered by God and each has unique gifts. We have prayed Proverbs 18:16 over their lives since they were in the womb "Your gift will bring you before great men!!" Harry III, Roman, and Gabrielle all walk in the wisdom and the admonition of the Lord. God is moving mightily in their lives.

As we serve God through Salem Family Ministries we continue to stand in the gap for families and people all over the world. We are mandated by the Lord to serve families, to bring restoration, and deliverance. God desires good, godly marriages. God desires marriages that children can look up to and say, "That's what I want to have when I grow up." We are here to serve those who are spiritual widows, who do not have a man to cover their home in the spiritual realm. I am well aware of the challenges women face in rearing children without a father, as I watched my wonderful mother rear our family.

Now, our family serves the body of Christ in all nations of the world. We are living examples of the mighty power of God to heal, restore, deliver, and set free. We are enjoying our destiny...and so can you.

It's too soon to give up . . . don't give up!

16

You Are Not Alone

Since I first began to openly share my story about depression, I have been amazed at the response. Harry and I have received letters from all over the country describing the pain people are experiencing from depression.

People from all walks of life have been impacted by depression... people that you would never think had any problems. Many people, including people who appear happy and successful on the outside, secretly suffer from depression.

The attacks of Satan are undermined when we have the courage to share our strength and pain by telling others. Because "we compare our insides with other's outsides", we are sure that everyone else lives a happy life...and we fear asking for help.

One of the lies that Satan always tells us is "You are the only one who doesn't have your life together...everyone else is happy...but look at you!" We must never believe this lie. The Bible describes many people who suffered from depression and despondency. David, "the man after God's own heart", suffered from depression. So refuse to believe this lie.

Remember, Satan will always attack us...but an attack is not a victory. A victory for Satan comes only when we accept the lies and live them out.

I've always said sometimes we get bruised and bloody in battle but what matters is who wins.

I'm going to close this book with a few testimonies of people who have suffered from depression and found victory. I've asked several of the people who have written to us to share their stories for your encouragement. If you have been healed and/or are believing God for your healing, please write and share with us. It really is too soon to give up.

Dear Cheryl and Harry,

I heard you on "The Road Show" today and wanted to take a minute to write you a note. Bless you and thank you for your honesty and openness regarding the challenges you have faced over the past two years. You're right, people don't want to know *what* to do; they want to know *how* to do it! I know your depression must be a difficult thing to share and does make you vulnerable to the listeners as you mentioned; however, *being so transparent brings people, myself included, hope and courage to fight.*

As a highly motivated, over-achiever, I have faced my own battle with depression and have had to come to grips with a chemical imbalance. I attended Rhema, worked in the sales department at Harrison House (selling your books)! I am considered by my friends to be very strong in the Word and in the Lord.

However, I have sometimes suffered from crippling depression and have been on a long journey to obtain answers and help for my situation. Self-condemnation became a way of life and I felt I should be able to *choose* life and *confess* my way out of depression. This became a self-defeating battle that only plunged me further and further into depression.

The past few years have brought many answers and victories as I am daily growing in God's grace. My medical doctor is a wonderful believer that has helped me in the physical arena. A Christian counselor has aided me in the emotional and spiritual area and my wonderful husband has been my best friend and has faithfully stood by my side. You mentioned applying the blood of Jesus to yourself and I have learned to do this as well with wonderful, cleansing results.

No, I am not where I want to be but I am growing daily, have new hope for the call of God on my life and am eager to see God's plans unfold for our family. You were a tremendous encouragement to me today as I listened to you.

I've always admired you and greatly respect your walk with the Lord and your ministry. I am sorry you have been through the dark valley of depression the last couple of years but it is obvious you are triumphing in Christ and I am confident this will add a tremendous dimension to your already powerful ministry. There are many spirit-filled believers caught in the depths of despair of depression. They need the gentle Shepherd, the healing, compassionate Jesus to take their hands and lead them out. Thank you for being one of His helpers.

God bless you!

Betsy

Dear Harry and Cheryl,

Thank you so very much for your recent letter and copy of Harry's book, "For Men Only." Also, thank you for taking time to update me on the progress of your new book on depression, "It's Too Soon To Give Up." I was so blessed to hear from you and so moved that you took time from your busy, busy life to write to me. Thank you. I am agreeing with you that your depression book will deliver people from the darkness.

My husband suffered with such bad depression that his counselor told him it was a miracle he survived. My two sons, Robert, 23 and Andy 19, also suffered from depression. Robert's battle was so intense that he talked about ending his life. I knew I had to get help.

In March of '96 I went to the "Women's Conference." I was sure that God was directing me to get to you so you could pray with me. I pushed through the crowd, like the woman with the issue of blood in the Bible, so I could talk to you. This is really against my nature...I usually stand back so others can receive prayer. In my heart I knew that you were the only one who had the anointing to free my family from the captivity of depression.

I'm happy to report that God answered our prayers. Our two sons are happier and more at peace than they have ever been in their lives. I have also seen a big difference in the direction they have in their lives. God has used your prayers to bring us peace.

Rob received a raise and the use of a company truck. (This was an answer to prayer because when he was so depressed he had to sell his truck due to financial problems.) Rob's attitude is brighter and happier than I have ever seen.

Andy got the job we have been praying for and his deep hurts from the past are being healed. He is like a new person!

I know your new book on depression will destroy the yoke of depression off millions of people.

Cheryl and Harry, thank you so very much for your prayers and time. We are a transformed family because of your prayers.

Your Servant In Christ,

Brenda

Dear Cheryl and Harry,

I was 32 years old when I first became ill. I am a business woman and the mother of three teens. Five years ago, I had a massive stroke. It left every voluntary muscle on the left side of my body paralyzed. It destroyed my sense of touch, taste, and smell. It also left me color blind to green and red. The stroke left me unable to handle any stress. I was told I would probably never walk again and I might have to consider living in a nursing home for the rest of my life.

I was a born again, spirit-filled Christian who chose to trust God's Word...because I, like you, knew that God was my only hope...I had no hope but in Him. With the Lord's help I was able to regain my strength and balance to stand and finally walk during the first year after my stroke.

On the outside, I appeared to be getting my life back together but on the inside I harbored grief and resentment. It wasn't long until depression had taken over my life.

Every week for nearly a year, I received treatment from a born again Christian counselor...but I couldn't shake my depression. Soon I lost the joy of the Lord that I had experienced in the first year of recovery. I fought depression and its sister spirit of suicide. For four years, I was filled with heaviness, anger, bitterness, resentment, and hopelessness.

When I attended your meeting, I was in terrible shape but God didn't leave me there. While at the meeting my depression lifted...I was completely healed. I felt the joy of the Lord as I had never experienced! At the meeting, I learned how to enjoy the presence of the Lord and how to stay in His presence and fellowship with Him. During this time, I came to feel God's leading to help others in the ministry. I can't tell you how exciting it is to see God at work in my life!

I wanted you to know that God has used you and Harry to help me. I thank God for each of you and your ministry.

Love

Diann

I feel fortunate to share in telling anyone who reads this book what a blessing Harry and Cheryl Salem are for anyone out there who is hurting. They can tell you about hurt, because they have been hurt and lived through some tormenting times and came out victorious. They are people of God and have been a great inspiration to our family here in Dallas, Texas.

Years ago, while in my early 40's, married almost 30 years to my dear husband at the time and the mother of three wonderful children, I found myself out of control. I was suicidal and I wanted to die. I drank myself out of my mind for three long hellish years. Talk about someone walking in darkness. That was me. Hopeless, lifeless, and very bitter. I hated anyone that tried to love me or get close to me. I was in bondage to the curse of drinking and depression due to the accumulation of all the rejection I had experienced in my life.

I myself came from a family of ten brothers and sisters.

Being raised with my grandmother since birth, I only knew my real parents and siblings through occasional visits, but I grew to love them. I lived for their constant approval, only to be cruelly rejected. I gave and gave love, but it was never returned. The rejuection ensued me turning into an alcoholic, retreating into my sorrow, and mentally abusing my loved ones. I was living a life of feeling defeated and beat down, insecure in so many ways. Satan and his demons came in and changed me from a loving human being into an angry, hurt, bitter and venomous woman to my husband and my children. My joy was completely gone. My attitude was bleak and desperate. I became a prisoner in my own home, making my bedroom as dark as possible and evil thoughts my refuge.

One day after turning on the the television I heard about a woman's conference and they invited any woman who was hurting to come. I said to myself "I'm a hurting person, I'm that person they're inviting." I then called my daughter and said "What do you think about going?" She of course, considered this an answer to her prayers. During the conference, I was healed and delivered from the demonic spirits of rejection, alcoholism and depression. When I returned to Dallas and my family, I was a new person, a new creation in Christ (2 Cor. 5:17). My world seemed a brighter place. I actually wanted to live again and tell the world about the awesome power of our Lord and Savior Jesus Christ. I realized that He created me and I was a "Somebody" in His eyes. I was always trying to be "Somebody" but always managed to feel like a "Nobody". After seeing all the hardships Miss America 1980 went through in her own lifetime and seeing that she still came out on top with the help of the Lord, I knew I could too, if I gave my hurts to God. "Greater is He that is in you, than he that is in the world!" When I went to Tulsa,

Oklahoma looking for help, I never dreamed I would return to Dallas a changed Woman of God myself.

I am now a "Warrior for Christ" serving our living God daily as a servant to the homeless, wounded single mothers, the drug addicts and the lost with no hope or direction in their lives. These are the people God has called me to reach out to and tell them the good news. I live to be used for other hurting people not only here in America, but throughout the nations if that's where the Lord leads. I'm in love with Jesus and I'm so full of joy today. I can't think of anything else I'd rather do than serve Him. It is important to always keep your self and your loved ones covered in constant prayer. Also, have intercessors pray with you and for you against Satan's attacks on a regular basis.

God will give you the hunger to know Him more intimately and to acquire the knowledge to ward off the evil one and his schemes for your destruction. The liar comes to steal, kill and destroy. He almost destroyed me and my family's lives, but the Good Lord reached out to me and saved me. Today I'm able to accept and love myself. I'm able to love my two daughters, Teri Rae and Angelina Kae, and my only son, Kris Edward the way their mother should have years ago. I'm also able to give my husband Eddie of 38 years the love and respect he deserves. I'm only able to do this after going through the fire...but not getting burned.

What's important is being set free from demonic oppression and possession and moving forward to the Higher Calling of God. Only he can provide emotional healing by washing our sins away and creating us into His image to use us as He has intended since being in our mother's womb.

I will always be grateful to Harry and Cheryl with my whole heart. God gave them to me to replace the blood family that rejected me. He wanted me to see the unconditional love of Christ shown as a member of the body of Christ. They will be family and friends in Christ forever here on earth and in heaven.

Angelina Irene Kemper
Angelina's Ministries
Dallas, Texas

Salem Family Ministries
Order Form • P.O. Box 701287 • Tulsa, OK 74170
918-298-0770 Fax 918-298-2517

Title	Price	Qty	Total
An Angel's Touch	$16.00	___	___
For Men Only	$ 7.00	___	___
A Royal Child	$ 7.00	___	___
The Mommy Book	$ 9.00	___	___
Warriors of the Word..	$ 5.00	___	___

Second in a series of children's action books. Also contains book #1, Fight In The Heavenlies

From Our Children to You (audio tape)	$10.00	___	___

Songs by Harry III, Roman and Gabrielle Salem

Making My Dreams Come True (audio tape).............	$ 8.00	___	___
Making My Dreams Come True (CD).......................	$10.00	___	___
Family Matters (2 tape audio)	$ 9.00	___	___
Male and Female (audio tape)	$ 5.00	___	___
Male and Female (video tape)	$15.00	___	___
Testimony On Abuse (video tape)	$15.00	___	___
Testimony On Depression (video tape)	$15.00	___	___
What Are You Tied To? (audio tape)	$ 5.00	___	___
What Are You Tied To? (video tape)	$15.00	___	___

Please call for more selections of teaching and music audio and video tapes.

Order Total ___ ___

Shipping and Handling	Order Total	Shipping
	$0.00 – 10.00	$3.00
	10.01 – 25.00	$4.00
	25.01 – up	$5.00

Subtotal _____

Donation to Salem Family Ministries _____

Grand Total _____

Payment Method ☐ Cash ☐ Check ☐Credit Card

Paying by Credit Card
☐ Visa ☐ MasterCard ☐ Discover

Credit Card # _____ Expiration Date _____

Signature _____

Send Order To:

Name _____

Address _____

City _____ State _____ ZIP _____

Phone _____

Dear Precious Reader;

If you have dealt with depression or are dealing with it now, we pray and believe with you for God to touch and heal your spirit, soul and body. We come into agreement with you for your total and complete healing to be manifested in your life.

Satan, get your hands off God's property! They don't belong to you and you have no right to torture them with these depression spirits. We rebuke you in Jesus' name. Stop it...that's enough!

Precious one, you are healed of the Lord. We call it so in Jesus' name. Today you are better. Today you are healed! Isaiah 60:1 is our Word confession over you today and every day in Jesus' name! (insert name in blanks below)

_____ arise from depression and prostration in which circumstances have kept you. _____ rise to new life! _____, shine (be radiant with the glory of the Lord), for _____'s light has come, and the glory of the Lord has risen upon _____!

You are above this spirit of depression. Now walk free from this day forth. No matter what you feel or what the circumstances look like, proclaim your liberty in Jesus' name! We agree with you this day _____ that you are free, delivered and healed!

Cheryl and Harry Salem